The WHITE ALBUM

This book is for Pat, Kelly & Alyssa – the best all-girl group ever!

THIS IS A CARLTON BOOK

Published by Carlton Books Limited 20 Mortimer Street London W1T 3JW

Copyright 2018 © Carlton Books Limited

A CIP catalogue for this book is available from the British Library.

ISBN 978-1-78739-187-1

Printed in Italy

10 9 8 7 6 5 4 3 2 1

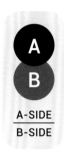

A-SIDE
B-SIDE

The WHITE ALBUM

Revolution, Politics & Recording:
The Beatles and the World in 1968

Brian Southall

CARLTON
BOOKS

CONTENTS

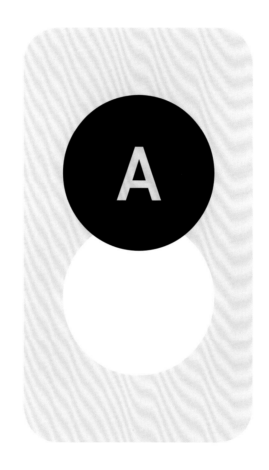

A-Side

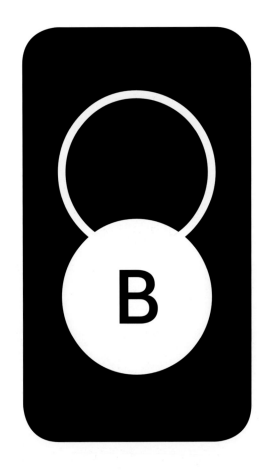

B-Side

CONTENTS

FOREWORD BY CHRIS THOMAS – PRODUCER ON *THE BEATLES*

Left: Seated on a red platform in front of the Maharishi Mahesh Yogi are (l to r) Ringo Starr, Maureen Starr, Jane Asher, Paul McCartney, George Harrison, Patti Boyd, Cynthia Lennon and John Lennon.

Right: John Lennon and Paul McCartney promoting their Apple companies in New York.

In 1968, at the age of 21, I realized that the only thing I wanted to do was become a record producer. George Martin, Ron Richards, John Burgess and Peter Sullivan had formed an independent production company called AIR London (Associated Independent Recording) and they offered me a chance to learn by giving me a six-month trial. I went to loads of sessions at Abbey Road, especially The Hollies, and then attended the first couple of months of the White Album. My job was to sit quietly at the back of the control room, suited and booted. ("Oh Chris! Would you like to clean your shoes?" George's wife, Judy, once enquired.)

I was there to learn the ropes from the masters, never having the slightest inkling of where this might lead. I certainly didn't expect to be making a contribution.

After three months of recording, George went on his summer holiday, something he had planned before the sessions had started. I came back from mine to be greeted by a tiny handwritten note from George.

"Dear Chris, I hope you had a nice holiday. I'm off on mine, make yourself available to the Beatles. Neil & Mal know you're coming down."

I don't think it was ever his intention that I should attempt to stand in for him – he just meant for me to carry on as normal. There was, however,

a slight miscommunication somewhere. When Paul arrived, he wanted to know why I was there, and gently invited me to produce them, telling me exactly what would happen if I was "no good".

Terrified? Nah...

Catatonic...

For five hours.

Eventually, I realized that if I screwed up it was highly likely that George Martin might also tell me where to go upon his return.

Taking the bull by the horns, a beautiful friendship formed. I stayed on the sessions until the end of the album, and even ended up playing on some tracks with George upstairs producing... us (?) Quite a lot happened in 1968.

Chris Thomas, 2018

INTRODUCTION

As night follows day – and so on – so 1968 followed 1967, and the hopeful hippie philosophies of peace and love gave way to organized sit-ins and uprisings… and music once again changed its tune to fit in with in the new mood.

It was undoubtedly the case that by 1968 life for a host of teenagers and emerging adults had taken many different turns and moved on in a variety of new directions. After all the excitement in 1967, with flower power, bells, kaftans and classic "psychedelic" songs such as 'Strawberry Fields Forever', 'A Whiter Shade Of Pale', 'Light My Fire', 'A Day in the Life', 'Penny Lane', 'Ruby Tuesday', 'Purple Haze' and 'See Emily Play', there was a new mood – and sadly, it was less colourful, less vibrant and less fun.

From being a trainee reporter on a newspaper in Essex – and being able to pin down where and when I first heard the glorious sounds of *Sgt Pepper* – I had moved on to being assistant sports editor of a weekly paper in Surrey.

This involved me leaving home for the first time and moving into a flat with NO record player... the family Dansette stayed at my parent's house. There was the radio, of course, but with a new job and all that went with it, my focus shifted from music and records to all things sporty.

In addition to my new journalistic responsibilities, which took me through the 1967–68 football season, I got engaged on the day that West Brom won the FA Cup. Even as an Aston Villa fan, being born and raised near Birmingham, this was still something to be celebrated as a rare and unexpected victory for the Midlands.

In the same month, with my new fiancée Pat, I went to Wembley to watch Manchester United beat Benfica and bring the European Cup to England for the first time. The tickets came courtesy of a raffle run by Kingstonian football club, one of the teams I covered and, bizarrely, it was only last year – nearly half a century on – that I found out that my brother was at the same match!

Before the new football season kicked off in August 1968, I had moved back to Essex to become sports editor of another local paper. It was reckoned at the time that I was the youngest sports editor in the country, and while that may have been the case – I had just turned 21 – I was certainly the cheapest sports editor in the land, earning less than £20 a week.

This was at a time when, according to the Office of National Statistics, the average weekly wage for a man over 21 in full-time manual employment was £22; a woman of the same age received £11 a week. When I did finally break through the £20 barrier at around Christmas time, I no longer received a weekly envelope stuffed with cash but was paid by cheque... and that meant opening my first bank account, which was something those of us who thought we were rebelling against the capitalist society really didn't want to do – except when the alternative was not getting paid!

This was also the year when the average house price in Britain was £4,200 (nearly $15,000 in the US); a new car would cost around £1000

($2,800 in America); a gallon of petrol was 5s.3d (28p) in Britain and 34 cents in the US; and a loaf of bread (sliced, unsliced, large or medium?) was 1s .6d (9p), and a pint of milk 3s .6d (17p).

It was the period when, for the first time, families in Britain were able to enjoy instant mashed potato, bounce on a space hopper and watch Basil Brush on television while playing with the new Hot Wheels toys and, if you were in America, you would have seen the famous golden double-arches 'M' logo for the first time, introduced by McDonalds in November 1968.

And depending on where you lived, you could pop along to your local rock venue – be it a club, theatre, cinema or town hall – and see the up-and-coming bands of the day. In the week that *The Beatles* album came out, it would have cost you 12s .6d (62p) to see Pink Floyd at the Crawdaddy club in Richmond, and 10s (50p) to catch either Jethro Tull at Mothers in Birmingham or Fleetwood Mac at the Locarno in Swindon. At the same time, my local hot spot – the Corn Exchange in Chelmsford – featured Geno Washington and the Ram Jam Band.

But in the midst of all this activity, I still can't pin down where and when the White Album came into my life. I have an original copy – sadly not an early numbered one – and writing this book

---

Left: Paul McCartney, Ringo Starr and George Harrison pose with cut-out John Lennon at the premiere of *Yellow Submarine* in July 1968.

"The music was there as an essential soundtrack to it all"

Brian Southall

(and listening to the album while doing so) has reminded me of the music, both good and bad.

It has been a joy to remind myself of the merits of 'Back in the U.S.S.R.', 'While My Guitar Gently Weeps', 'Blackbird', 'Rocky Raccoon', 'Julia', 'Helter Skelter' and 'Revolution 1' in particular, alongside the strangeness of 'Wild Honey Pie' and 'Revolution 9', and the obvious commerciality of 'Ob-La-Di, Ob-La-Da' and 'Goodnight'.

Obviously, like all things Beatles, it had a place and a role in my formative years and, although it's not up there alongside *Sgt Pepper*, *Revolver* or *Abbey Road*, the White Album will be linked forever with all that went on around the world in 1968 – the tragedies, the demonstrations, the protests, the advances and the achievements. And once again, the music was there as an essential soundtrack to it all.

Brian Southall, 2018

Right: The Beatles found their way to Old Street tube station in north London during their 'Mad Day Out' photo shoot in the capital with photographers Don McCullin and Stephen Goldblatt.

"...THE MUSIC WAS BETTER ON THE DOUBLE ALBUM BECAUSE I'M BEING MYSELF ON IT"

John Lennon

"IT IS ANOTHER STEP... BUT IT'S NOT NECESSARILY IN THE WAY PEOPLE EXPECTED"

Paul McCartney

"AFTER *SGT PEPPER* THE NEW ALBUM FELT MORE LIKE A BAND RECORDING TOGETHER"

George Harrison

"I AGREE WE SHOULD HAVE PUT IT OUT AS TWO SEPARATE ALBUMS; THE 'WHITE' AND THE 'WHITER' ALBUM"

Ringo Starr

"As a social document of the time this was the Beatles' most important record – a reflection of where they were and where they were at."

Journalist and author Mick Brown

"I just thought it (*The Beatles*) wasn't a good title because it was confusing – it could have been a compilation of Beatles things."

Journalist and author Ray Connolly

"Personally I think it's their least inspired effort and I find it difficult to listen to."

Beatles engineer Geoff Emerick

"Beatles albums are a major part of my life and always will be but the White Album is not one of them. It was too long and you had to get through a lot of padding to get to the good stuff."

Leader of Cockney Rebel Steve Harley

"The versatility of *The Beatles* was very attractive – they mixed it all up and had fun tracks."

Photographer Gered Mankowitz

"When it came out, as it was a double, it was confusing and difficult to grasp initially as there was so much of it… this was really exploratory and long."

Roxy Music guitarist Phil Manzanera

"I thought we should probably have made a very, very good single album rather than a double."

Beatles producer George Martin

"It was a big album with a lot of songs to choose from and some are my absolute favourites and some are my least favourites."

Beatles engineer, producer and musician Alan Parsons

"We had a blast. It was fun. They were great to work with."

Beatles, Roxy Music and Sex Pistols producer Chris Thomas

"Whatever else it is or isn't, it is the best album they have ever released, and only The Beatles are capable of making a better one. In short it is the new Beatles record and it fulfils all our expectations of it."

Founding editor of *Rolling Stone* magazine Jann Wenner

A-Side

THE BEATLES

The birth, growth and eventual emergence of four young men from Liverpool as the world's most popular and best-remembered pop group of all time is a well-told story.

John Lennon was in the Quarrymen, a hopeful, local skiffle group playing in and around Liverpool, when he met Paul McCartney at a local garden fête in July 1957. As the group changed direction to pursue a rock 'n' roll dream, George Harrison was recruited to the line-up during 1958.

After a brief turn as Johnny & the Moondogs, the band recruited Stuart Sutcliffe to give the group the highly original line-up of four guitarists and no permanent drummer. Under the name the Silver Beetles, they took on more dates and, eventually, added drummer Pete Best to the line-up, just in time play the first of a series of residences, in August 1960, in the clubs of Hamburg, where they would return to regularly until December 1962.

In fact, in just over two years, they played a total of 279 nights in four different clubs in Germany's major sea port, and the experience prompted Harrison to remark, "I'd have to say with hindsight that Hamburg bordered on the best of Beatles times."

By 1961 Sutcliffe had left, deciding to stay in Germany, and the new four-piece Beatles came to the attention of local Liverpool businessman Brian Epstein, owner of the city's NEMS record store. After seeing them perform on 'home territory' in the city's famous Cavern Club, he took them under his wing, signing The Beatles to a five-year management contract effective from February 1, 1962.

However, despite the band's popularity as a "live" act – they were regulars at the Cavern,

and around the north west of England – Epstein was anxious to get his "boys" a record contract and, following a failed audition with Decca on New Year's Day 1962, he found his way to the attention of rivals EMI. A chance visit, in May, to the company's HMV record store in London's Oxford Street, to get an acetate made from the Decca audition tape, resulted in a meeting with the music publishers Ardmore & Beechwood, also owned by EMI and housed in the HMV store. From there, he was recommended to Parlophone record producer George Martin.

Suitably impressed by what he heard, Martin offered Epstein and his group a standard EMI recording contract valid for one year with three one-year options. The deal gave The Beatles the chance to earn 1d (.41 pence) per double-sided disc, which would be split five ways between the group and Epstein.

The group subsequently made their debut in Abbey Road Studios on June 6, 1962 and recorded four tracks under the direction of Martin's assistant, Ron Richards. By the time they returned in September, The Beatles had a new drummer as Ringo Starr was brought in to replace Best; the line-up, augmented by drummer Andy White, who was on stand-by as nobody in the studio had heard Starr play, recorded the Lennon and McCartney song 'Love Me Do'.

The group's debut single peaked at No. 17 in the UK chart and, in early 1963, The Beatles set about making their debut album. In one extraordinary session lasting over 12 hours,

ten songs were recorded in Abbey Road and, alongside the two sides from their first single and the hit follow-up 'Please Please Me' and 'Ask Me Why', comprised the group's debut album *Please Please Me*. It knocked Cliff Richard off the top of the UK chart and was eventually replaced – after 30 weeks – by their second long-player, *With The Beatles*.

Life would never be the same again for John, Paul, George and Ringo as hit record followed hit record, and eventually, America caught "Beatle-fever" when in 1964 The Beatles had six US No. 1 singles. Sell-out tours, million-selling discs, international music awards and even MBEs (Members of the British Empire) all came their way as Beatlemania took over the world.

But in August 1966 The Beatles broke fan's hearts by performing their last-ever live concert, in San Francisco's Candlestick Park. Their eleven-song set brought the curtain down on nine years of performing live, during which time, under various guises, they had played over 1,400 shows.

The 'fab four' now turned to the studio as the place where they would make their music and, after recording for over 700 hours during a five-month period – at a record cost of £25,000 – they emerged, in June 1967, with the all-conquering album *Sgt Pepper's Lonely Hearts Club Band*. With its ground-breaking artwork, and despite

Right: John Lennon, Paul McCartney and George Harrison share a microphone during the White Album sessions at Abbey Road studios.

"I thought of nothing else but rock 'n' roll"

John Lennon

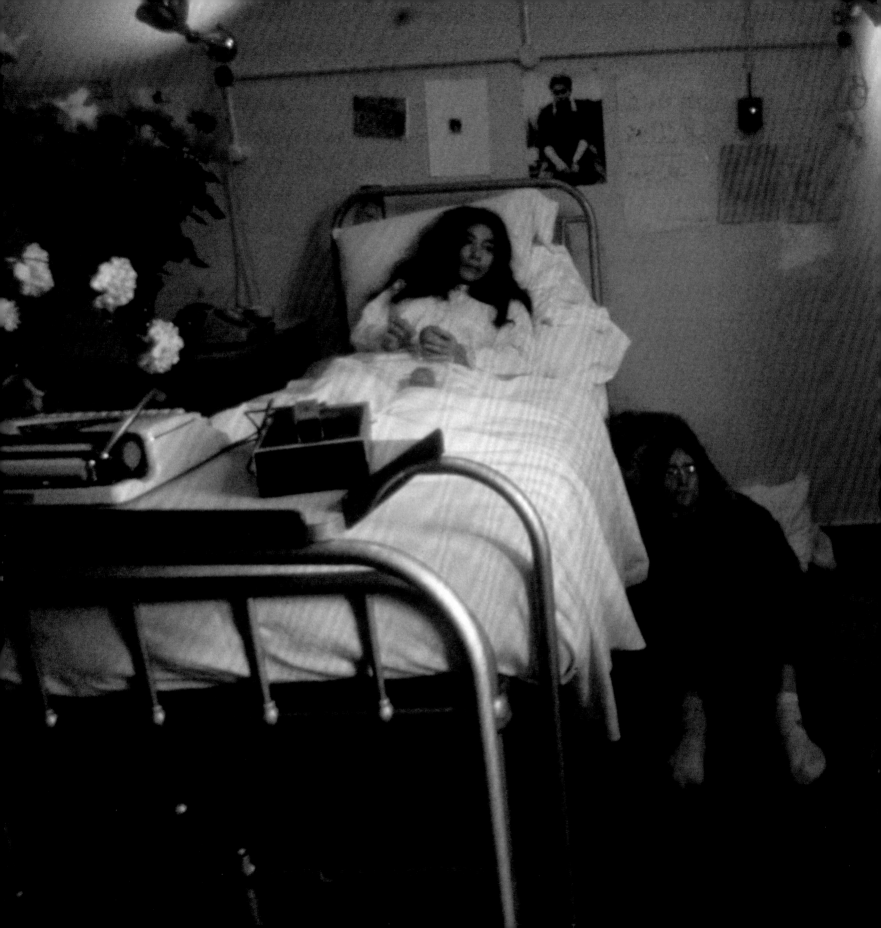

having no hit singles, the 13-track "concept" album passed the 2.5 million sales mark in three months and topped the UK and US album charts for a combined total of 38 weeks.

While this was a new peak for The Beatles, they had to deal with the death of their manager Brian Epstein in August 1967, and the slow-burning fuse of disharmony which was creeping into the band's previous sense of togetherness. Even so, over the next three years, The Beatles issued three more chart-topping albums – *The Beatles* (or the White Album), *Abbey Road* and *Let It Be* – and started a host of Apple companies before finally falling out over who should run their business affairs.

For author and journalist Ray Connolly, The Beatles' Apple concept was right in one area. "It was mostly absurd but Apple Records was great – they had the right ear and knew what they were doing with music." However, the man who wrote the screenplays for the films *That'll Be the Day* and *Stardust*, was less than impressed with Paul McCartney's theory.

"I remember Paul trying to explain about Western Communism and thinking 'is this a new form of economic history that I've not heard about?' I didn't think it was going to work. Nobody was running the shop, they weren't interested and were very quickly bored." Around this time, there was also a newspaper story that The Beatles were planning to launch a budget label, issuing records that would sell for 10s (50p), with American poet Allen Ginsberg named as a potential artist.

Derek Taylor worked for The Beatles between 1964 and 1965 before taking over as PR man for the group and Apple in 1968. In December of that year, he admitted in a press interview, "We certainly haven't brought about a revolution in the music business. We've failed in that. But all the other revolutions this year have failed too."

Left: John Lennon at Yoko Ono's bedside in St Charlotte's Hospital following her miscarriage in November 1968.

"When we got together we all had an amazing, positive feeling about being in the band full-time"

George Harrison

The arrival of Allen Klein to look after Lennon, Harrison and Starr, while McCartney favoured his soon-to-be father-in-law Lee Eastman to do the job, led to the final legal break-up of The Beatles in March 1971 when a High Court Judge agreed to McCartney's petition to dissolve the partnership known formally as Beatles & Co.

Watching as his company's most famous and successful act began to fall apart was EMI chairman Sir Joseph Lockwood, who did his best to keep things on an even keel. "I tried to stop it falling apart and had no trouble with Paul but Yoko was a problem and there seemed to be no solution than for The Beatles to break up."

He was also concerned about the choice of Klein to be involved with the group. "He was a terrible problem. He wanted to change the contract they had signed in 1967, and I said we would be happy to change parts of it. But he wouldn't agree to anything so I told him to get out."

An hour later, Lockwood, who died in 1991 after 20 years at the head of EMI, received a phone call of apology from Klein and adds, "Later in some magazine interview he said he thought I was wonderful but that everybody else at EMI was shit."

Through his work with the Rolling Stones and Jimi Hendrix, photographer Gered Mankowitz was closer than most to the pop-music scene in 1968 and he saw it as an era of change. "Artists like the Beatles and the Stones were evolving, gaining more creative control but losing business control as they got bigger and more global. Allen Klein was developing his grip on both of these groups in a very Machiavellian way."

With this in mind, and maybe with a sense of what lay ahead, The Beatles perhaps placed as the last full track on the final album they ever recorded together a song called 'The End'. Written by McCartney, it suggests that the love you take is equal to the love you make – a lyric that Lennon observed was "a very cosmic, philosophical line."

However, the story of The Beatles seemingly has no end as their music continues to live on, way past their demise as a creative force. New releases – including the mid-nineties hit singles 'Free As A Bird' and 'Real Love' – compilations, anthologies, re-mastered re-issues and, ultimately, downloads have all served to keep The Beatles alive and loved nearly 50 years after they fell apart.

Right: Joining the group Grapefruit (front) to announce their signing to Apple Publishing are (l to r) Brian Jones, Donovan, Ringo Starr, John Lennon, Cilla Black and Paul McCartney.

JOHN LENNON

Even though he was the first of The Beatles to play music before any sort of an audience, was John Lennon the leader of the band? He certainly founded the Quarrymen, recruited Paul McCartney, gave George Harrison the nod and later helped get Pete Best replaced by Ringo Starr. He also came up with the idea of changing The Beetles – the band's name after the Silver Beetles – to The Beatles.

And it was Lennon who steered his bands – whatever they were called – towards rock 'n' roll, the music that influenced him more than anything else: "I thought of nothing else but rock 'n' roll." However, the arrival of McCartney as a player and budding songwriter gave the duo a new edge as they set about creating the music that would see The Beatles transcend the boundaries of pop music.

His talent also extended to art and literature and, two years into the Beatles' success story, he published a collection of his drawings, verse and rhymes. *In His Own Write* sold over 100,000 copies and was followed by a second successful volume, *A Spaniard in the Works*.

However, there was also a controversial side to Lennon, and his comments in 1966 that The Beatles were "more popular than Jesus" led to the group's records being banned and burned in some places in America. Within a year the group retired from touring and settled on life in the studio but, three years on, The Beatles were finished and Lennon, together with new wife Yoko Ono, set about creating new music while campaigning for world peace.

At the same time, he made hit albums such as *Imagine, Some Time in New York City* and *Walls and Bridges* but died tragically young when he was murdered in New York – the city that had been his home for a decade – on December 8, 1980, aged just 40. Within weeks of his death, Lennon's single '(Just Like) Starting Over' – released two months earlier – became a posthumous No. 1 in both the UK and the US.

Above: John Lennon – musician, artist, author and campaigner.

Right: John Lennon and Yoko Ono first met at an art exhibition at the Indica Gallery in London in 1966.

PAUL McCARTNEY

It was Paul McCartney's ability to play American rocker Eddie Cochran's 'Twenty Flight Rock' which so impressed John Lennon that he was an immediate shoo-in to join the Quarrymen back in the late fifties.

"That's what got me into The Beatles," said the bass player and songwriter, and it also led to the creation of the most extraordinary songwriting team which changed the face of 20th-century popular music. From the early days of writing songs such as 'Love Me Do' and 'I Saw Her Standing There', Lennon-McCartney became the credit on more than 200 songs published by Northern Songs, the company they shared ownership of with manager Brian Epstein and music publisher Dick James.

As The Beatles continued to produce million-selling singles and albums featuring the songs – many composed individually but always jointly credited – written by the two most prolific members of the band, McCartney ventured into creating film soundtracks and experimental electronic music – reckoned by those that heard it to be "layers of Beatles overlaid on Beethoven" – in addition to writing for and producing other artists.

He became the complete music-business impresario with his own production company and the acquisition of numerous song catalogues, including musicals such as *Grease* and *A Chorus Line*, while his own song, 'Yesterday' is the most recorded song in music history with over 2,000 cover versions.

Cited as the wealthiest man in British music, McCartney has a record number of Ivor Novello song-writing awards, a Lifetime Grammy Achievement award, and he became

Sir Paul in 1997. While he once admitted that he could "sit back now and be a company director," McCartney's work ethic has driven him, since his 1970 debut solo album, to produce a further 35 studio albums, including pop, classical and soundtracks, plus eight live collections.

His 1977 Wings single 'Mull of Kintyre' topped the British chart for nine weeks and became the biggest-selling single in the UK, overtaking The Beatles 1963 hit 'She Loves You'.

Below: Paul McCartney on his way to catch a flight to New York.

Right: Paul McCartney – musician, composer, music publisher and businessman.

GEORGE HARRISON

A life in music probably began for George Harrison when he displayed his guitar-playing skills to McCartney and Lennon on the top deck of a Liverpool bus, and was recruited to join the Quarrymen.

"When we got together we all had an amazing, positive feeling about being in the band full-time," Harrison recounted but, throughout the swinging sixties, as The Beatles swept all before them to rule the pop world, the lead guitarist took on the role of the 'quiet' Beatle.

While his playing was never in doubt, he and drummer Ringo Starr were always in the shadow of the group's two main creative forces – Lennon and McCartney. In the face of such strong competition, Harrison struggled to get the songs he had composed considered for The Beatles' albums: he managed just three out of the 68 songs on the group's first five.

However, before the group finally split up, Harrison created songs such as 'Taxman', 'Blue Jay Way', 'While My Guitar Gently Weeps' and 'Something' and then went off to become the first of the group to 'go solo' with projects such as *Wonderwall* and *Electronic Sound*. He was also the first band member to return to touring when he joined Delaney & Bonnie for dates in Denmark in late 1969.

He continued his run of 'firsts' by becoming the first ex-Beatle to top the charts, thanks to his album *All Things Must Pass* and the single 'My Sweet Lord', while at the same time remaining committed to Eastern culture, philosophy and the Hare Krishna movement – and producing films such as Monty Python's *The Life of Brian*, pursuing his passion for motor racing and joining the renowned Traveling Wilburys.

In November 2001 Harrison died from cancer, aged 58, and his ashes were scattered in the sacred Indian rivers, the Ganges and Yamuna, as was his will.

Above: George Harrison shares the limelight with a 'Blue Meanie'

Right: George Harrison – the 'quiet Beatle' who was the first to go solo in 1968.

RINGO STARR

As the last man to join the line-up of the most famous band of all-time, Ringo Starr had to put up with protests from fans in Liverpool about him replacing Pete Best despite his three fellow Beatles welcoming him to the fold.

Described by Paul McCartney as "the greatest drummer in our eyes," Starr – real name Richard Starkey – built his reputation with the band Rory Storm and the Hurricanes before switching to The Beatles in August 1962, just in time to attend the group's second session in Abbey Road Studios.

Never a prolific songwriter or lead vocalist, Starr was given brief moments in the spotlight, performing lead vocals on songs such as 'Boys', 'I Wanna Be Your Man', 'With a Little Help from My Friends' and two of his own compositions – 'Don't Pass Me By' and 'Octopus's Garden'. Respected as the oldest member of the group, Starr went down in history as the first person to quit The Beatles when he walked out of a recording session in August 1968. He returned to the fold a few days later, and even took on the role of peacemaker as the group fell into disarray.

At the same time, he turned to movies as a new outlet, appearing in the film *Candy* and with Peter Sellers in *The Magic Christian*, before releasing his debut solo album, *Sentimental Journey*, in 1970, closely followed by the hit single 'It Don't Come Easy' and eventually forming his own long-standing All-Starr Band in 1989.

Often to referred to as the "world's wealthiest drummer", Starr has endured a degree of sniping about his ability as a musician but his reputation was enhanced in 2011 when readers of *Rolling Stone* magazine voted him the fifth-best drummer of all time behind the likes of Dave Grohl, Neil Peart, Keith Moon and John Bonham.

Above: Ringo Starr made his solo acting debut as a gardener in the sex farce film *Candy*.

Right: Ringo Starr was named the fifth best drummer of all-time in a magazine poll.

BRIAN EPSTEIN

Was he the fifth Beatle? It was a title he was given in respect of his efforts to turn The Beatles into the most successful pop act the world had ever seen. However, Liverpool-born Brian Epstein only found his niche in the music industry after being thwarted in his ambitions to be a dress designer or an actor.

After returning to the family's furniture business, he moved to the NEMS (North East Music Stores) his father had opened in central Liverpool, where he ran the record department, and began to see opportunities in Britain's burgeoning pop business.

Persuaded to go to the Cavern Club to see an emerging act called The Beatles, Epstein struck up a relationship with the group and took over their management in 1962 – in return for 10% of income up to £1,500, and 15% on anything above that.

A meeting with producer George Martin earned the group a recording deal with EMI's Parlophone label and, with music publisher Dick James, a company called Northern Songs was formed to handle the group's compositions. Epstein then created his own NEMS Enterprises to manage The Beatles and other Liverpudlian acts such as Cilla Black, Gerry and the Pacemakers, and Billy J Kramer and the Dakotas. He also bought the Saville Theatre in London's West End and turned it into a successful music venue.

Even though he was the architect of their unprecedented success, Epstein's career as The Beatles' manager was by no means without its flaws. A disastrous merchandising deal in America, in which The Beatles only earned 10%, meant that questions began to be asked about his future in the role.

Even though he was considered dedicated and honest, Epstein was viewed by some as too naïve for the cut-throat world of pop music, and doubts were raised as to whether The Beatles would retain him after his contract expired at the end of 1967.

In the end, it was all academic as 32 year-old Epstein was found dead at his home in London on August 27, 1967 as a result of an accidental overdose of barbiturates.

Right: Brian Epstein went from managing a record store to become manager of The Beatles.

"The Beatles were disintegrating slowly after Brian Epstein died"

John Lennon

GEORGE MARTIN

The man who was destined to become arguably the most famous record producer in the world had ambitions to be a professional pianist after serving in the Royal Navy, studying at the Guildhall School of Music and working for the BBC.

However, George Martin chose to become part of EMI's Parlophone label in 1950, and worked with artists such as Peter Ustinov, Humphrey Lyttelton and Peter Sellers before enjoying his first UK chart-topping record thanks to The Temperance Seven's 'You're Driving Me Crazy' in 1961.

Within a year, he had met, recorded and signed four young men from Liverpool who would change his life forever. Together, The Beatles and Martin became an inseparable creative force and, over a seven-year period, he was involved in producing more than 30 international hit singles and close to 20 chart-topping albums for the "fab four" – and was also dubbed the fifth Beatle.

Martin's workload at Abbey Road involved producing hits for acts such as Cilla Black, Gerry and the Pacemakers, Billy J Kramer and the Dakotas, and the Fourmost, but a dispute over royalties led to him leave EMI in 1965 and form his own AIR (Associated Independent Recording) studios.

Martin's experience as a both a producer and musician was an essential element in The Beatles' recording process, as John Lennon acknowledged in 1971, explaining, "I can remember what George Martin did. He would translate it." While he never abandoned The Beatles, the group gradually became more at home in the studio and, according to Paul McCartney, "started to take over."

But he was on hand right up until the end, as the five-man team of Martin and The Beatles produced *Abbey Road* as a fitting finale to their long and successful studio partnership. Through the release of compilations, anthologies and re-issues, Martin continued to be involved with the work of The Beatles until he retired in 1996, the same year that he was knighted for his contribution to music.

In March 2016, at the ripe-old age of 90, Sir George Martin died at his home in Wiltshire and McCartney stated categorically, "If anyone earned the title of the fifth Beatle it was George."

"If anyone earned the title of the fifth Beatle it was George"

Paul McCartney

Right: Sir George Martin, producer of the Beatles' music for over 30 years.

THE WHITE ALBUM

After making what was generally considered to be the first concept album, The Beatles were faced with the problem of how to follow their multi-million selling, award-winning homage to the psychedelic sixties.

If *Sgt Pepper* represented a new Beatles – a studio band free from the rigours of touring and promotion – what followed came as a mighty shock to millions of the group's fans around the world.

The four men from Liverpool had long ceased to be the "fab four mop-tops" who created "Merseybeat" but now they were heading into new waters – and they were sailing solo. While *Sgt Pepper* was essentially a group effort, The Beatles were slowly drifting apart, both musically and personally, and that would be a test for their legion of fans.

As a devoted mod who viewed The Beatles as an "uncool guilty pleasure", student Liz Woodcraft recognized a change. "We didn't appreciate how interesting they were musically and by the time I got to Birmingham University (in 1968) people were thinking they were cool and groovy after *Sgt Pepper.*"

Trainee teacher Lynne Timmington was also aware that something was happening with her favourite group. "Before it had all been about enjoying the music but then they became such individual personalities and I was getting fascinated by them."

Legendary music presenter Bob Harris was also well aware of what The Beatles had achieved up to this point. "[They] had revolutionized the pop scene in ways more profound than just record-breaking singles sales," and similarly Alan Thompson, now a radio, television and computer retailer in Essex, identified with the band's significance back then. "The Beatles were for a long time the backdrop to our lives, and the release of a new album was a very big moment for people."

Left: Ringo Starr, George Harrison and Paul McCartney pose for the photographers at the premiere of the film *Yellow Submarine*.

Above: Ringo Starr does a spot of amateur camerawork during the filming of *Candy*.

"When we started I don't think we thought about whether the White Album would do as well as *Sgt Pepper*"

George Harrison

In fact, the next Beatles album would not see the light of day until late November 1968 but, following the death of their manager Brian Epstein in 1967, John Lennon, Paul McCartney, George Harrison and Ringo Starr had become masters of their own destiny. "They could now do what they wanted because there was nobody saying 'are you sure about that?'" is writer Ray Connolly's assessment of the situation.

American university lecturer and Beatles author Ken Womack agrees that losing their manager was a major moment for the group. "Their own professional lives were still reeling from the untimely death of Brian Epstein, which led to a power vacuum in the bandmates' ecosystem," and in later years Lennon admitted, "The Beatles were disintegrating slowly after Brian Epstein died."

Tony Bramwell was a life-long friend of The Beatles from Liverpool, who worked in Epstein's management company and saw at first-hand the arrival of a different Beatles. "John, Paul, George and Ringo were anxious to make a fresh start. As individuals all four were bursting with talent, and couldn't wait to get started on separate projects which had been impossible for them to pursue as part of a touring group."

Following the success of *Sgt Pepper* and their own extraordinary inventiveness in the studio, The Beatles returned to Abbey Road on February 3, 1968 after more than two months away and, within three days, they had finished recording the A-side of their first single of the New Year.

'Lady Madonna' was followed by 'Hey Jude', which was started in Abbey Road on July 29 and completed at Trident Studios on August 1, and The Beatles had two new international No. 1 singles to their name. And in between the two hit singles, they had begun work on their next, as yet untitled, album.

Talking to *New Musical Express (NME)* in July about their recording plans, Harrison admitted that they had plenty of material, saying, "We have about forty [songs] in all and we don't know yet which ones we'll use," while McCartney added, "I hope it will get made quicker than the *Sgt Pepper* album."

In February all four Beatles plus wives, girlfriends and assorted friends, including Beach Boy Mike Love, actress Mia Farrow and her sister Prudence, and singer Donovan, arrived in India to spend time at the retreat of the Maharishi Mahesh Yogi on the banks of the River Ganges.

While it was essentially intended as a trip to meditate and take stock of their position, it also proved to be a hugely creative period for all four Beatles. "All the stuff on the White Album was written in India," said Lennon. "We got our mantra, we sat in the mountains eating lousy vegetarian food and writing all those songs."

Breaking it down, he went on to explain, "Paul must have done about a dozen. George says he got six and I wrote fifteen. And look what meditation did for Ringo – after all this time he wrote his first song." Armed with all the material they might need to make an album, all four Beatles had returned from India by the

middle of April and began preparing themselves for the task ahead.

Love, a founding member of the Beach Boys, spent much time with The Beatles in India and saw what they were achieving. "The Beatles time in Riskikesh could not have been more productive", he says. "They wrote nearly 40 songs, including all 30 that were on the White Album."

"When we started I don't think we thought about whether the White Album would do as well as *Sgt Pepper*," says Harrison. "I don't think we ever really concerned ourselves with the previous record and how many it had sold."

While the band would obviously still play together in the studio, the songs they were going to record were, as Harrison explains, different. "There was a lot more individual stuff and for the first time people were accepting that it *was* individual."

Long-time friend and confidante of the group, Peter Brown suggests that the need for them to be seen as individuals was at the heart of their problems. "By the time of the White Album sessions, the Beatles' working relationship had disintegrated to the point where the only way for them to get anything accomplished in the studio was for one of them to wrest control for

Right: Paul McCartney (and Martha the sheepdog) with Apple signings The Black Dyke Mills Band who made 'Thingumybob' in 1968.

Following pages: During their day being photographed around London The Beatles hid among the flowers in the garden at St Pancras Old Church.

the recording of his own composition while the others played 'back-up band'."

However, when The Beatles returned to Abbey Road Studios at the end of May, there was a new technical development on the horizon, as the studio was on the verge of installing eight-track machines to replace the existing Studer J37 four-track machines. "The first eight-track machines couldn't do recording in the same way as we did," explains the studio's then technical engineer Ken Townsend. "So I went to the Studer factory in Switzerland because they wanted to ensure that the machine they brought out could do the things we wanted."

When the new machine was finally delivered, it still wasn't operational, and Abbey Road's own tape-machine expert, Francis Thompson, set about modifying it. "He had just about finished his work by the time The Beatles wanted to use it," recalls Townsend, who also confirms that the new machine didn't change things that much. "They did have a new toy but The Beatles didn't take to eight-track straight away because the machine couldn't do what they wanted to do and lots of the tracks on the White Album were recorded on four-track – they got better results by using two four-track machines and bouncing between them."

But there was also another new arrival in the studio, which had a more immediate impact – Yoko Ono. Recalling how things developed, engineer Geoff Emerick said, "John brought her into the control room of [studio] Number Three at the start of the sessions. She was always there after that."

For the other band members, the presence of Lennon's girlfriend slowly became a negative issue, as Harrison recounted. "Yoko just moved in. At first it was a novelty but after a while it became apparent that she was always going to be there and it was very uncomfortable because this was us at work."

Pointing out that his own wife Maureen and Harrison's girl-friend Pattie Boyd were irregular visitors to the studio, Ringo Starr added, "Suddenly we had Yoko in bed in the studio. It

created tension because most of the time the four of us were very close. That was where *we* were together." Paul McCartney, too, was moved to say, "Now John had to have Yoko there. I can't blame him – but it was fairly off-putting having her sitting on one of the amps. We were The Beatles, after all, and here was this girl..."

Author Ray Coleman commented that The Beatles were "flabbergasted" that Lennon allowed Ono not only to be in the studio but also to comment on their work. "Only the four of them plus George Martin had ever been allowed

that privilege." Even the usually cool and calm George Martin was moved to suggest that "it was no longer the happy-go-lucky foursome – fivesome with me – that it used to be," while long-time Beatles technical engineer Townsend simply said, "Yoko being there didn't help a lot."

Ray Connolly, who first met The Beatles when he was invited on to the *Magical Mystery Tour* coach trip, spent some time in the studio during the making of their new officially titled album *The Beatles* and noticed things were not as they should have been. "How irritating must

it have been for Paul and George to have Yoko in the studio? She was manipulative but she could also be very nice. John was always re-inventing himself and was seduced by things, and he wanted to be an intellectual and she gave him that."

Left: Donning a hat and cravat combination, George Harrison turns out for the premiere of *Yellow Submarine* at the London Pavilion.

Above: George Harrison and Pattie Boyd smile for the cameras at the Cannes Film Festival.

A

Speaking nearly a decade after the release of the White Album, Harrison confirmed that The Beatles were making the album at a time when some of the band were thinking of leaving. "I know the first time for me, which was the most depressing, was during the White Album. It was a problem making a double album because it takes so long."

For Abbey Road engineer Geoff Emerick, who began working with The Beatles in 1962, the White Album sessions were far from enjoyable. "They were angry. I had no idea what it was they had to be angry about, but they had a definite chip on their collective shoulder when they returned to the studio to begin work on the new album."

Working "in the midst of all this turmoil and bad feeling was not a good omen," recalls Emerick, who says, "The Beatles were bringing their problems into the studio for the first time... the entire atmosphere was poisonous."

All this would eventually lead to Emerick deciding he wanted no further part in proceedings, as Beatles' author Kenneth Womack has observed. "The first casualty was engineer Geoff Emerick, who couldn't stomach all of the infighting as [George] Martin and the Beatles attempted to find their way."

Speaking some years after his time as stand-in producer, arranger and session player on the

Below: Look this way! The media were always out in force to get a picture of The Beatles.

Right: John Lennon and Yoko On at the launch party for Lennon's 'You Are Here;' art exhibition in July 1968.

White Album, Chris Thomas was at pains to point out, "We had a blast. It was fun. They were great to work with." As he spent more time with The Beatles, he also noticed how they behaved as a group and as individuals. "It was interesting to me that they were definitely individuals until all four of them were together and then you noticed that they became The Beatles. That was weird.

"If you were talking to any of them individually you were just talking to that one person but once the other three were there then suddenly that person became very different. There was a sort of invisible thing between them."

While he never expressed publicly any concern or unhappiness with the progress of the recording, Martin did go on holiday midway through the sessions, which surprised Womack, author of *Maximum Volume: The Life of Beatles Producer George Martin: The Early Years, 1926–1966*. "Martin created an uncomfortable, albeit ominous distance by retreating to the rear of the control booth, where he would pick apart a large Cadbury chocolate bar as he pored over a stack of newspapers."

While describing the White Album as "a nearly 180-degree turn from their work during the previous year on *Sgt Pepper*," Womack further concluded, "By September he [Martin] went AWOL for three weeks in a poorly-deployed power play that forced him to carry out a host of post-production duties." Interestingly, Ken Townsend, a long-time associate of Martin's in Abbey Road, concludes, "It wasn't odd that George went on holiday as he had arranged for Chris Thomas to come in and replace him."

Thomas himself has never seen any hidden agenda in Martin's absence. "The suggestion that George hired me in order for him to go on holiday is odd because nobody knew how long the album was going to take. George booked his holiday thinking the album would be finished by the time he went away."

While Martin's return from his vacation was marked by a session on October 1 in Trident Studios, and he was back in Abbey Road within a week, which was around the time that Jeff Lynne, later the leader of the Electric Light Orchestra, visited the studio. It was probably on October 10 when a song by Lennon and one by McCartney were both completed: "There was John Lennon and George Harrison sitting there, and George Martin conducting the orchestra. They were doing this song called 'Glass Onion'."

Then Lynne, who over 25 years later would co-produce The Beatles' singles 'Free as a Bird' and 'Real Love', wandered off to catch another session. "I went into this other studio where there was a session going on with Paul McCartney and he was doing 'Why Don't We Do It in the Road?' I wish he'd been doing something a bit better, but you can't have everything."

Townsend also recalls that this was a time when each of The Beatles arrived at the studio separately and in their own time, which was not how it was in the beginning. "Originally they used to come to the studio all together with Mal Evans [their roadie] but now it was different."

And having someone in the studio during the recording sessions was a complete turnaround for a group whose sessions were notoriously private and attendance was by invitation only. "If they saw someone in the control room they didn't know they'd stop and wait and find out who it was. They didn't like anyone they weren't aware of being in the control room and looking down on them," adds Townsend

However, irrespective of what was going on in and around the studios, The Beatles knew that an album had to be made and so they returned to the studio to begin creating something that, for American Womack, would turn out to be "one of the most remarkable of The Beatles' masterworks," even though, in his opinion, "the unsettling nature of its creation resonate through almost every track."

Left: Paul McCartney paints Donovan's face in Riskikesh during the Indian 'Holi' spring festival of colour.

Right: Apple signing Mary Hopkin and Paul McCartney play together watched by TV and radio presenter Pete Brady.

SIDE ONE

'BACK IN THE U.S.S.R.'

The album's opening track was started on August 22 and finished the next day – without Starr. The Beatles' drummer walked out on the band after being criticized by McCartney over a fluffed tom-tom fill during the recording and spent the next two weeks on a yacht in the Mediterranean.

Undeterred, McCartney sat in on drums for the recording of his song, with Lennon and Harrison possibly adding their own drum contributions, which finished with a tape of an aeroplane taking off and landing, acquired from London Airport.

When he was creating the song in India, McCartney shared it with Beach Boy Mike Love, who claims he suggested that it should be "a Soviet version of 'Back in the USA'", the 1959 hit song by Chuck Berry.

Admitting that it was his "take-off" of Berry's song, McCartney explained, "I just liked the idea of Georgia girls and talking about places in the Ukraine as if it was California." And to recognize Love's contribution, The Beatles added Beach Boys-style harmonies courtesy of Lennon and Harrison.

Music writer Mick Brown heard the opening track as a teenager in London and recalls that back then "the West was a society in upheaval" and suggests the song "was very symbolic of the West turning to the East in search of some sort of spiritual enlightenment, a respite from Western consumerism."

Regularly covered by Alice Cooper – "we always do 'Back in the U.S.S.R.' in our shows" – the song caught the ears of the music reviewers, with *NME's* Alan Smith describing it as "a fantastic piece of screaming excitement"

and *Melody Maker's (MM)* Alan Walsh adding that the opening track "has a tremendous rock beat with searing jet aircraft noises."

Despite the praise, 'Back in the U.S.S.R.' managed to upset some Americans who, concerned about the Vietnam War and the Cold War, suddenly questioned the politics of The Beatles. Meanwhile, McCartney described his composition as "a hand across the water song" aimed at the Soviet Union.

'DEAR PRUDENCE'

Prudence was Prudence Farrow, the younger sister of actress Mia Farrow (star of *Rosemary's Baby*), and both of them were among the group attending the Maharishi Mahesh Yogi's meditation classes alongside The Beatles.

Something of a shy recluse, Prudence rarely joined in the group sessions in India and, according to McCartney, this inspired Lennon to write the song. "John wrote the song for her because she had a panic attack and couldn't come out of her chalet."

A self-confessed meditation fanatic, Farrow was never played the song by Lennon or told about it, and only found out when Harrison mentioned it as they were all leaving India. "I didn't hear it until it came out on the album," said Farrow, who added, "It was a beautiful thing to have done."

Work on the album's second track began in Trident Studios in London's Soho on August 28 and, over the next two days, it was completed with the help – on vocals, handclaps and tambourine – of roadie Mal Evans, Apple singer Jackie Lomax and McCartney's cousin John who was in town on a visit. The Beatles chose to go to Trident because Abbey Road was full, as

Ken Townsend recalls. "We had Pink Floyd and other acts in, and once a studio was booked that was it – we didn't throw anyone out, not even for The Beatles who probably tried to get in."

Fifteen years after the track first appeared, it became an unlikely British top-ten hit for UK punk outfit Siouxsie and the Banshees.

'GLASS ONION'

"That's me just doing a throwaway song, á la Walrus, á la everything I've ever written," was Lennon's explanation for 'Glass Onion', which was picked up by Ray Connolly, who wrote in his *Evening Standard* review at the time, "They would appear to be deliberately trying to cover as many of their musical influences without becoming intellectually condescending."

Interestingly in light of all the claims that the songs on the White Album were all individual compositions by each of the Beatles, McCartney went on record to confirm that, while "it was John's song", they did join forces occasionally. "We still worked together, even on a song like 'Glass Onion', where people think there wouldn't be any collaboration."

The whole song was Lennon reacting to what he called the "gobbledegook about *Pepper"* where people searched for (and apparently found) hidden meanings in the group's lyrics, and even claimed to hear messages when the music was played backwards. He was creating images in poetry by referring to earlier work by The Beatles plus a place in Liverpool known as the Cast Iron Shore, and the name he had in

Right: George Harrison, Ringo Starr and Patti Boyd take time out to meditate at the Rishikesh retreat in February 1968.

mind for Apple signings The Iveys, who chose to go with Badfinger instead.

It was recorded at Abbey Road on September 11, when 34 takes were completed in a session running from 7pm until 3.30am the following morning. After three more sessions, the track was finished on September 16 when a recorder – probably played by McCartney – was added.

'OB-LA-DI, OB-LA-DA'

Having picked up the title phrase and the line "life goes on" from Nigerian conga player Jimmy Scott-Emuakpor, McCartney found himself walking around the Indian meditation camp strumming his guitar and singing 'Ob-La-Di, Ob-La-Da'.

He admitted it had nothing to do with meditation but was a "little story about Desmond and Molly", set in a West Indian reggae style, which was dubbed "white ska". *MM's* Walsh declared it was "great stuff all about sunshine and 'de market place'." He also suggested that it was a song that "is going to be a smash for somebody", and that somebody

"I decided to write a song based on the first thing I saw upon opening the book – as it would be relative to that moment"

George Harrison

turned out to be Marmalade, who hit No. 1 in the UK charts in 1969.

It was a song which Lennon apparently disliked intensely and also got bored with during recording, as the sessions spread over eight days between July 3 and July 15. During that time, session musicians contributed brass, electric piano (courtesy of ace session man Nicky Hopkins) and percussion – and the name of the bongo player was listed simply as J. Scott.

The track also features a particularly loud piano contribution from Lennon, as McCartney recalls. "John was late for the session. He sat down at the piano and instantly played the blue beat style intro. It turned us on and turned the whole song around. He and I worked on the vocals and I remember the two of us in the studio having a whale of a time."

At the time, McCartney wanted the track to be released as a single, but had to wait until 1976 when it was released in America and peaked at No. 49 in the US chart.

'WILD HONEY PIE'

Lasting just 53 seconds, 'Wild Honey Pie' was a piece of improvisation from McCartney that was started and finished at the end of an overnight session which began at 8pm on August 20.

Describing it as a "fragment of an instrumental which we were not sure about", he contributed overdubbed vocals, guitars and drums in a one-man performance, which he

considered "very home-made; it wasn't a big production at all."

According to *NME's* Smith, it arrived as "a brief piece of headache music," while *Rolling Stone* founding editor Jann Wenner considered it a "nice tribute to psychedelic music and allied forms."

'THE CONTINUING STORY OF BUNGALOW BILL'

So who was Bungalow Bill? It seems he was Richard Cooke III, an American college graduate who travelled to India to visit his mother Nancy during her studies with the Maharishi. At some point, mother and son took off on a big game hunt during which he shot a tiger.

Back at the ashram, Nancy Cooke spoke excitedly about her son shooting a tiger and that sowed an idea in Lennon's head for a song. "It was written about a guy who took a short break to go shoot a few poor tigers and then came back to commune with God," explained the Beatle, who also confirmed where the name came from. "There used to be a character called Jungle Jim and I combined him with Buffalo Bill. It's a sort of teenage social-comment song and a bit of a joke." He seemingly added in Bungalow because all the accommodation at Rishikesh were bungalows.

Recording was all done in one day – October 8 – and, during the three takes, Yoko Ono sang the solo line "not when he looked so fierce", the first lead vocal by any female

on a Beatles record. Sometime producer Chris Thomas, who would go on to work with Pink Floyd on *Dark Side Of The Moon* and produce Roxy Music, the Sex Pistols, Elton John and Paul McCartney, added mellotron. "This was one of the first things we did when George came back," explains Thomas. "It was just mad as I was now playing live in The Beatles and George Martin was producing."

Bizarrely, Cooke was not aware of the song until he began receiving postcards from friends, who somehow recognized him from the song, asking 'Hey, Bungalow Bill, What did you kill?' *MM's* Alan Walsh astutely suggested that the whole thing "could be interpreted as a protest against killing or hunting."

'WHILE MY GUITAR GENTLY WEEPS'

The recording of Harrison's most famous contribution to the new Beatles album was spread over three months, and involved an incredible 44 takes stretching from Harrison's solo vocal and acoustic guitar demo through to final a version involving a guitar legend.

It was in his mother's house in Warrington, Lancashire that Harrison was inspired to create the song when he was picking through *I Ching,* the Chinese Book of Changes, and came across the line 'gently weeps'. "I decided to

Left: Paul McCartney, Jane Asher, Maureen Starr and Ringo Starr about to board their plane to fly to India to join the Maharishi in February.

Left: Cilla Black and Paul McCartney rehearse his song 'Step Inside Love' which became her first top ten hit for two years.

Above: George Harrison (centre) celebrates his 25th birthday in Rishikesh with the Maharishi, Ringo Starr, Maureen Starr and Patti Boyd.

write a song based on the first thing I saw upon opening the book – as it would be relative to that moment."

Disappointed with the reaction of Lennon and McCartney to his song – "they weren't taking it seriously" – Harrison continued to update versions, which included the very first eight-track recordings in Abbey Road, on September 3, using the new machine, which had been modified and was just about ready to use.

Two days later, Starr returned to the studio to re-join The Beatles, and found his drum kit covered in flowers as a welcome-home message. His first session was on another re-make of Harrison's song and, speaking to *Crawdaddy* magazine in 1977, George explained the problems he had getting a song onto a Beatles album. "I had a little encouragement from time to time but it was very little. They never said 'yeah that's a good song'. When we got into 'While My Guitar Gently Weeps' we recorded it in one night and there was such a lack of enthusiasm. So I went home really disappointed because I knew the song was good."

Determined to get his song right, Harrison brought Eric Clapton in to finish the track. "George drove me over to Abbey Road Studios where he was recording," recalls Clapton. "When we arrived he told me that they were going to record one of his songs and asked me to play on it." That was on September 6 and, in just one take, the man who was on the point of leaving Cream got it right. "I thought it was fantastic but John and Paul were fairly non-committal, but I knew George was happy. It felt like I had been brought into their inner sanctum."

For Harrison, the song also represented an important development in the publishing of his music. 'While My Guitar Gently Weeps' was the first song of his to be credited to his new music-publishing company Harrisongs, which he formed at the end of his association with Northern Songs. Unfortunately, some early pressings of the new album mistakenly credited the song to Apple Music.

Left: Ringo Starr shows off a replica Grammy award to producer George Martin (l) and engineer Geoff Emerick.

Right: John 'the rocker' Lennon as Elvis (or maybe Gene Vincent) at a fancy dress party.

'HAPPINESS IS A WARM GUN'

What their fans and the critics read into the lyrics of their songs always fascinated and amused The Beatles, and Lennon's completed work – the sum of three different unfinished songs – was no exception.

For singer Steve Harley and his friends it was about only one thing. "To me and my mates, no matter what anyone said, it was about heroin. We were quite happy to believe it was about heroin which we never indulged in but we knew was dangerous."

Some radio stations took the same view and banned it, while others refused to play it because they saw some sort of sexual symbolism in the song. However, for the composer, the song's source and title was the cover of a magazine he found in the studio. There was a picture of a smoking gun on the cover and an article entitled "Happiness Is a Warm Gun In Your Hand," which Lennon picked up on. "I thought it was a fantastic, insane thing to say. A warm gun means you've just shot something."

Beginning on September 23 and ending two days later, the track was recorded and re-recorded, under the guidance of replacement producer Thomas, until there were a total of 70 takes to work from. "Good and solid" was *NME's* opinion of the song, which apparently both McCartney and Harrison viewed as their favourite track on the album, and one Lennon liked too – "I consider it one of my best. It's a beautiful song and I really like all the things that are happening in it."

SIDE TWO

'MARTHA MY DEAR'

If he took the title from the name of his three-year-old Old English sheepdog Martha, there is still some uncertainty as to whether McCartney was singing to her or about her. It has been suggested that, in fact, it was a song written for and about a girl who had been a muse to the musician, or that it referred to his ex-girlfriend Jane Asher, who had broken off their engagement in July 1968.

And if there are doubts about the inspiration for the song, there are some further doubts as to whether any of the other Beatles played on the song, written by McCartney as a piano exercise. "This started life as a piece you'd learn as a piano lesson," explained McCartney. "It's quite hard for me to play, it's a two-handed thing, like a little set piece."

Describing the a song as a "communication of some sort of affection but in a slightly abstract way," McCartney went into Trident Studios on his own on October 4 and 5 to record the song with the help of 14 musicians who added brass and strings during a three-hour session on day one.

'I'M SO TIRED'

Life in India revolved almost entirely around meditation which left Lennon unable to sleep at night as he struggled with the alcohol-free – and drug-free – environment. Three weeks into his stay he wrote 'I'm So Tired' about sleepless nights and the lack of cigarettes and drink.

"Being tired was one of John's themes. I think we were all pretty tired, but he chose to write about it," said McCartney, and while *MM* picked up on the song's "hard blues sound building with organ and guitar," *NME*'s man suggested that the song would become famous for "Mr Lennon's sympathy with addicted tobacco smokers, expressed in the gem 'curse Sir Walter Raleigh, he was such a stupid git'."

Renowned as a fast worker when it came to working on his own songs in the in the studio – on session tapes he could be heard urging, "the red light's on, let's go, let's make a record" – Lennon started and finished this song in one day, albeit during a mammoth 16-hour session, which began in Abbey Road on October 8.

'BLACKBIRD'

If there was uncertainty as to whether 'Martha My Dear' was a solo Beatle recording, there is no doubt about the song 'Blackbird' which was written by McCartney, not in India but at his farm in Scotland before he brought it to Abbey Road on June 11.

It was started and finished in 32 takes during a six-hour session when McCartney's double-tracked vocals were accompanied by his acoustic guitar and the ticking of a metronome. The finishing touch was the sound of a bird, which had been recorded early in the morning after an all-night session by putting a microphone outside the studio. "There was a bird singing in a pear tree early in the morning, and when Paul played the tape to me I told him it was a thrush not a blackbird," explains Ken Townsend. He is also sure that the bird song on the record did not come from the studio's sound effects library – "although there might have been one there."

The inspiration for 'Blackbird' – which *NME's* Smith described as "music to be sad by" – remains a subject for conjecture, with some suggesting it came from the composer hearing a blackbird, while others believe it was inspired by race riots in America and the assassination of Martin Luther King in the April.

However, McCartney has said that the tune came from Bach's 'Bourée in E minor' and his early guitar practice. "The original inspiration was from a well-known piece by Bach which George and I had learned to play at an early age; he was better than me actually." The Beatles also confirmed that Bach was one of The Beatles' favourite composers – "we felt we had a lot in common with him."

Graham Nash, whose group Crosby Stills & Nash were rejected by The Beatles' Apple Records, recalls his reaction to hearing the song. "When we heard 'Blackbird' we jumped all over it with three-part harmony. It's one of those tunes we've sung steadily over the years."

'PIGGIES'

In a song he described as "social comment", Harrison took a swipe at the middle classes by using a term usually identified in the sixties as a derisory American slang expression for the police.

It was described by reviewer Connolly as "Orwellian", and he also suggested it would become a children's favourite. In his book *Animal Farm*, George Orwell had identified pigs as the tyrants who ruled society.

Recorded in 11 takes on September 19, it featured all four Beatles and a harpsichord

Left: Paul McCartney takes the lead to conduct The Black Dyke Mills Band.

played by Chris Thomas. He'd discovered the instrument in Abbey Road's Studio One and then moved the session from Studio Two in order to use it on the track, along with McCartney's bass creating the sound of a pig grunting. Three weeks later, eight string players added violins, cellos and violas.

In 1971 the song took on an air of notoriety when Charles Manson, leader of the American cult responsible for eight murders in Los Angeles in August 1969, revealed that his 'family' had seen the words of the song as a reference to the white establishment. When they scrawled the words 'Death To Pigs' and 'Pig' in their victims' blood, Harrison's song became notorious, although the composer explained, "It was nothing to with America policemen or Californian shagnasties."

'ROCKY RACCOON'

Written by McCartney during his month-long stay in India, 'Rocky Raccoon' is a song he described as "quirky, very me", and one for which he adopted a cowboy style with the main character, who was originally named Rocky Sassoon, resembling Western folk hero Davy Crockett.

"I like talking blues so I started off like that, then I did my tongue-in-cheek parody of a Western and threw in some amusing lines," explained McCartney, who apparently sat down on the roof of an ashram in Rishikesh with

Above: Donovan takes time out to relax during his trip to India with The Beatles.

Right: Maureen and Ringo Starr lead the way across a footbridge in India ahead of Paul McCartney and Jane Asher.

Lennon and Donovan, who helped out with ideas for the song.

Recorded in one session involving ten takes on August 15, it featured The Beatles plus George Martin on honky-tonk piano. Alan Smith in the *NME* reckoned the song was a twenties-style "singalong standout," which could be a hit single for somebody. It never was, although American singer Richie Havens' recording remains a memorable version.

'DON'T PASS ME BY'

Between 1963 and 1969 The Beatles issued nine albums and not one of them featured a song written by Starr. He had featured as a co-writer with the other Beatles on the track 'Flying' from the *Magical Mystery Tour* album, but 'Don't Pass Me By' was his solo debut as a songwriter.

According to the composer, the song was written in his house as far back as 1964 and long before the trip to India. "I was sitting around at home. I was fiddling around on the piano... and 'Don't Pass Me By' arrived." However, when it was started in Abbey Road on June 5, it had the working title of 'Ringo's Tune', which became 'This Is Some Friendly' before it turned into 'Don't Pass Me By'. After six takes it was finished, apart from the piano introduction, which was added nearly six weeks later in mid-July.

"It was great to get my first song down, one that I had written," says Starr. "It was very exciting for me and everyone was really helpful."

The mixing session for this track took place on June 6, which was when disc jockey Kenny Everett was allowed into the studios to interview The Beatles for his BBC Radio 1 show, broadcast on Sunday, June 9. He left with two jingles – one featuring Lennon and McCartney and another with Harrison and Starr – plus a new version of 'Strawberry Fields Forever'.

Right: George Harrison is joined by actors Rita Tushingham and Michael York for a sitar session at the EMI studios in Bombay.

'WHY DON'T WE DO IT IN THE ROAD?'

Described at the time by Connolly in the *Evening Standard* as one of McCartney's "rock/shout numbers", it was also an almost solo effort from the composer, which he recorded in Studio One with Abbey Road's leading technical engineer, Townsend.

"That's my claim to fame," says Townsend, who retired as the chairman of EMI Studios in 1996 after working at Abbey Road for over 40 years. "They were doing their own things and Paul said he had an idea for a song and wanted to go to another studio." Moving into Studio One on October 9, when it was set up for a classical session with Yehudi Menuhin the following day, McCartney and Townsend completed 'Why Don't We Do It in the Road?'

Left: Ringo Starr promoting the film Yellow Submarine.

Bottom: Paul McCartney take timeout in India with long-time Beatles' assistant Mal Evans.

Right: Yoko Ono and john Lennon on their way to Marylebone Magistrates court on drug charges in October.

"It was Paul's solo guitar and vocals and I set up a four-track machine to record it," recalls Townsend. "We did five takes and the next night we added eight strings on the final take, which lasted until 7.30 in the morning." They then added Starr's drum track on October 10.

With its risqué title, the song was inspired by the sight of two monkeys copulating in front of McCartney in the Indian jungle. "The song was just to pose that question. 'Why Don't We Do It in The Road?' was a primitive statement to do with sex or to do with freedom really. I like it, it's just so outrageous that I like it."

'I WILL'

McCartney was again spending time with the British folk singer Donovan in India, and 'I Will' was a song which apparently came after a day of meditation. "We were just sitting around and I played him [Donovan] this one and he liked it and we were trying to write some words," recalls McCartney.

However, it seems that whatever words they came up with didn't suit the song, as McCartney came up with a new set of lyrics. "I wrote my own set in the end; very simple words, straight love-song words really. It's still one of my favourite melodies that I've written." According to MM's Walsh, it was "Paul at his sweet best singing a pretty little song."

The song was recorded in a session that began at 7pm on September 16 and ran until 3am the next day and, during that time, three Beatles – George was not involved at all – laid down 67 takes, which involved the composer on acoustic guitar, Starr on maracas and cymbals, and Lennon tapping out the rhythm with a piece of wood.

'JULIA'

Talking about the idea that he was the balladeer while Lennon was "the shouter", McCartney once pointed out that 'Julia' was about Lennon's mother and was "a very sentimental piece."

It was also the only solo recording done by Lennon during his career with The Beatles.

Julia Lennon was the person who taught her son to play the banjo and introduced him to rock 'n' roll before she was tragically killed in a road accident in 1958, and this song was the first direct reference to her in any of his songs. It also makes mention of his new partner, Yoko Ono, as the 'ocean child' – Yoko means 'child of the ocean' in Japanese.

The song – described by *NME* as "a potential *Pepper* track with counter harmonies and a slight eeriness" – was the last song to be recorded for the album when Lennon accompanied himself on acoustic guitar during just three takes on October 13.

SIDE THREE

'BIRTHDAY'

Side Three of The Beatles first-ever double album opened with a song which McCartney made up in the studio on September 18. Having arrived before everyone else, he sat at the piano and played what producer Thomas describes as "the Birthday riff."

From McCartney's initial thought of "why not make something up," the riff developed into a song and, when the other Beatles arrived, they all threw in contributions, although recording was halted while everyone went to McCartney's house in nearby Cavendish Avenue to watch a film. "I had mentioned to Paul about *The Girl Can't Help It* being on television," says Thomas, adding, "The idea was start the session earlier and then all nip round the corner to Paul's house, watch the film and go back to work."

The Girl Can't Help It was an American film from 1956, which starred Jayne Mansfield alongside Eddie Cochran, Gene Vincent, Little Richard and Fats Domino, and was described by McCartney as "the greatest music film."

When everyone returned Abbey Road, Pattie Harrison and Ono were recruited to join The Beatles in adding backing and, after a total of 20 takes done in one day/night session, 'Birthday' was finished. In later years, Lennon went on record to declare, "It's a piece of garbage."

'YER BLUES'

Considered by many to be among the most depressing songs ever written by Lennon, 'Yer Blues' was completed in sessions covering two consecutive days in August. Work began in a

side room alongside Studio Two on August 13 – when 17 takes were recorded – and completed the next day in the actual studio.

Described by *NME* as "hard solid stuff not without humour", 'Yer Blues' was created at a time when Lennon was considering his life, both in the context of The Beatles and outside the group; they had stopped touring, their manager was dead and he was on the verge of ending his marriage.

As part of the unofficial super-group Dirty Mac – with Eric Clapton and Keith Richards – Lennon performed the song at the *Rolling Stones Rock 'n' Roll Circus* in December, and again at a festival in Toronto the following year.

'MOTHER NATURE'S SON'

While McCartney found the inspiration for this song in a lecture about nature given by the Maharishi in India, it was actually written in his father's house in Liverpool. "Visiting my family I'd feel in a good mood, so it was often an occasion to write songs," says McCartney.

Considered by Connolly to be one of the "several very good pure Beatle songs" on the album, it represented McCartney's love of the countryside and a 1947 song recorded by Nat King Cole called 'Nature Boy' – "I've always loved that song," the composer once admitted.

Left: George Harrison arrives back in London after his trip to record in India in January 1968.

Above: John Lennon wearing the talisman necklace he later gave to Apple Electronics boss Alex 'Mad Alex' Mardas.

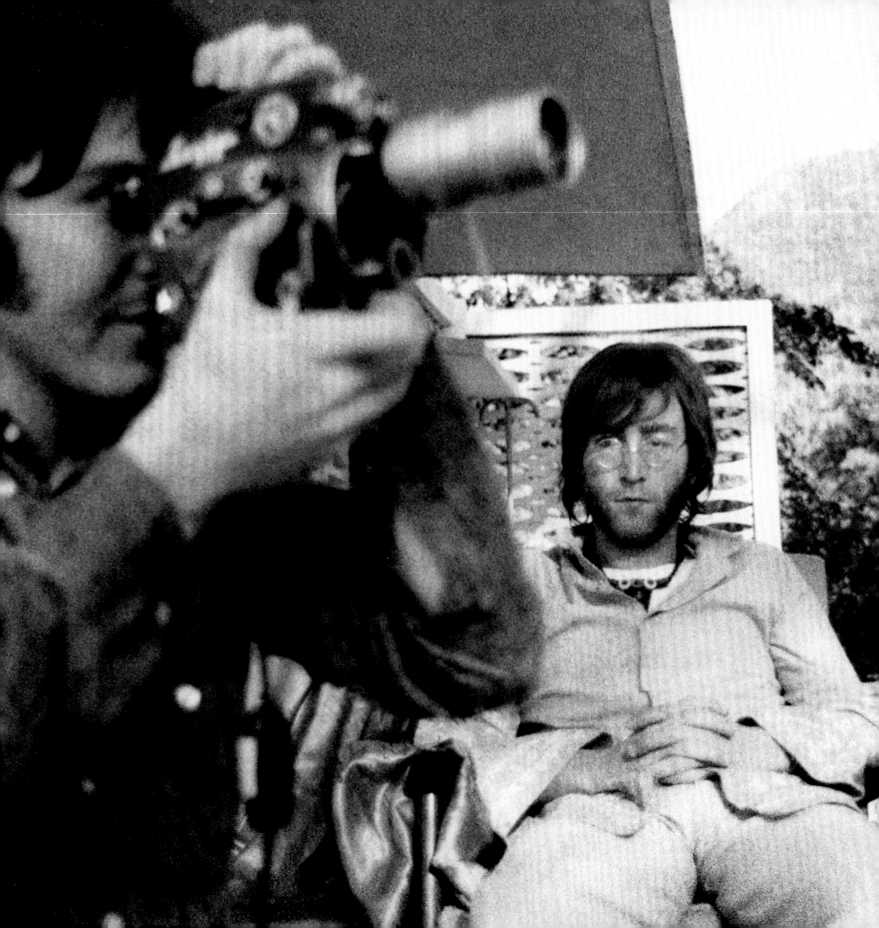

Once again it was McCartney on his own in the studio on August 9, when he completed 25 takes in an all-night session, taping his vocals and acoustic guitar. Just under two weeks later, timpani and brass were added to complete 'Mother Nature's Son'.

'EVERYBODY'S GOT SOMETHING TO HIDE EXCEPT ME AND MY MONKEY'

This was a song that began life in a session on June 26 when it was listed as 'untitled' and The Beatles ran through rehearsals but kept none of the recordings. These were replaced the next night when the song – still down on the recoding sheet as 'untitled' – came together in eight takes featuring double lead guitar, hand-bells and a Brazilian chocalho (a wand with cymballettes attached).

More work was done on July 1 before, during a final session on July 23, Lennon added a totally new vocal that, according to witnesses, he wanted to be "different". The song was written by Lennon in response to criticism in the British media of his relationship with Ono. "Everybody seemed to be paranoid except for us two... everybody was sort of tense around us," he once explained, although McCartney was concerned about drugs. "John started talking about fixes and monkeys, and it was harder terminology which the rest of us weren't into."

Referring to his bandmate's use of heroin at this time, McCartney added, "It was a tough period for John but often that adversity and that craziness can lead to good art, and I think it did in this case."

'SEXY SADIE'

Lennon and Harrison stayed in India for a week after McCartney left, and it was during that time that a rumour spread around the camp in Rishikesh that the Maharishi had made a sexual advance towards one of the American women guests.

Although there was very little evidence and nothing was ever proven, Lennon took it very seriously, and on his return to England, apparently told McCartney that the Indian mystic was "just a bloody old letch just like everybody else." In fact, Lennon was so upset that he decided put it all down in a song.

"John wrote 'Sexy Sadie' to get it off his chest," said Harrison, who added, "I don't think Maharishi ever made a pass. He didn't seem like the kind of guy who would." When Lennon left with Harrison he was singing a song naming the Maharishi and what he was rumoured to have done, but Harrison, intervened, telling him, "You can't say that, it's ridiculous." And it was Harrison who came up with the name Sexy Sadie.

McCartney said later, "George persuaded John to change the title... to protect the innocent. I think George was right. It would have been too hard."

In the album reviews written at the time, it was apparent that nobody made the connection between Sadie and the Maharishi, as they assumed the song was about a girl who, according to *MM*, "made a fool of everyone."

Recording 'Sexy Sadie' was spread over a month – between July 19 and August 21 – and involved The Beatles in over 100 takes before Lennon was satisfied.

'HELTER SKELTER'

It seems that a review of The Who's single 'I Can See for Miles' or an interview with its composer Pete Townshend in which the record was reckoned to be "the loudest, most raucous rock

'n' roll, the dirtiest thing they have ever done" was what drove McCartney to create the song 'Helter Skelter'.

"Just that one little paragraph was enough to inspire me; to make me make a move" he said. "I wrote 'Helter Skelter' to be the most raucous vocal, the loudest drums et cetera et cetera." The process of recording the song began on July 18, with Martin at the controls for three takes, which were soon abandoned and replaced by work done on September 9 – without Martin, who had gone on holiday.

He left a note for Chris Thomas, which told him to "make himself available to the Beatles", but, unfortunately, he didn't tell the group of the new plan and, according to Thomas, "it took a while for the Beatles to accept me."

Whatever Thomas imagined doing during his time in Beatle sessions –"I thought I'd just hang out and help make the tea" – taking over from Martin was not one of them. "I never anticipated producing a Beatles track – 'make yourself available to The Beatles' doesn't say have a crack at producing them. I might have be a warning about racial conflict in America.

Dismayed by Manson's association with his song, McCartney said, "It was frightening because you don't write songs for those reasons," while Lennon commented, "All that Manson stuff was built around George's song about pigs and Paul's song about an English fairground. It has nothing to do with anything. He's [Manson's] barmy, he's like any other Beatles fan who reads mysticism into it."

Daily Telegraph writer Mick Brown agrees that Beatles' songs were the subject of much analysis, particularly during the psychedelic sixties, as people searched for hidden meanings. "I'm sure lots of people who took lots of acid were receiving lots of messages from lots of Beatles songs."

'LONG, LONG, LONG'

Harrison's third song on the new album was started when he scribbled the lyrics in a 1968 diary, using the name 'It's Been a Long Long Long Time', which was still the working title when The Beatles began work on the number on October 7.

In an all-night session lasting over 16 hours, they ran through 67 takes of the song, which was inspired by the chords Bob Dylan used on his song 'Sad Eyed Lady of the Lowlands' on his 1966 double album *Blonde On Blonde*. In addition to guitars, drums and organ, an extra sound was discovered and left in, as Thomas recalls. "There's a sound near the end of the song which is a bottle of Blue Nun wine rattling on top of a Leslie speaker. We thought it was so good that we set the mics up and did it again."

The song was finished on October 9 when Thomas added piano and Harrison decided to shorten the title to 'Long, Long, Long', which was chosen to close the Side Three of the album.

done some auditions for artists, but I'd never actually done a session; so my first sessions were undoubtedly The Beatles."

And the 21-year-old studio trainee remembers the moment he became a "producer". "Paul walked in and asked what I was doing there. I explained that George Martin said it was OK for me to be there, and Paul said,

'Right if you want to produce us you can, if not you can f*** off.' I just thought 'what's going on'."

When it was released, the song, according to McCartney, "unfortunately inspired people to evil deeds"; Charles Manson, the man involved in the multiple murders in Los Angeles in August 1969, claimed he was inspired to order the killings by 'Helter Skelter', which he took to

Opposite: Ringo Starr captured on film (again) at the opening of the film *Yellow Submarine*.

Above: John Lennon and George Harrison take time out and relax on the banks of the River Ganges.

A

SIDE FOUR

'REVOLUTION 1'

The Beatles began work on their new album on May 30 with a 12-hour afternoon/evening session when 'Revolution' (without any number) was started, and 18 takes were completed with the song running for over ten minutes.

"The slow version of 'Revolution' on the album went on and on, and I took the fade-out part and just layered all this stuff over it," said Lennon, who added, "I did a few mixes until I got one I liked."

The final version of the song, completed on June 21, brought Lennon into a debate about the title word at a time when riots and protests were taking place all around the world – including London. Speaking about his songwriting partner's political leanings at the time, McCartney says, "He doesn't really get off the fence in it. He says you can count me out, in, so you're not actually sure... but it was an overtly political song about revolution and a great one."

Unsure of his position when it came to a revolution, Lennon used the words "count me out, in" on the slow, bluesy version of 'Revolution 1', which opened Side Four of the White Album

while the faster version, used as the B-side to 'Hey Jude' and recorded in July, had Lennon singing simply "count me out." It was this version that Lennon wanted to be released as the A-side of the first Beatles single on Apple, but he lost out when McCartney and Harrison voted for 'Hey Jude'.

'HONEY PIE'

As a self-confessed fan of old-time music hall, McCartney says he "very much liked that old crooner style, the strange fruity voice that they used." He was also influenced in this by his father Jim, who played ragtime music in local bands around Liverpool.

Talking about 'Honey Pie', which was assumed to be a tribute to his father, McCartney said "My Dad's always played fruity old songs like this and I like them. I would have liked to have been a 1920s writer because I like that top hat and tails thing."

He also admitted that it was "another of my fantasy songs" in which he was "writing to an imaginary woman across the ocean, on the silver screen, who was called Honey Pie." Reminiscent of 'When I'm Sixty-Four' from *Sgt*

Pepper, it was considered by *NME* to be "another of the commercial hit tracks of the set."

Recording was started at Trident Studios on October 1 – with Martin back from holiday – and three days later in Abbey Road, seven musicians – five saxophonists and two on clarinet – added parts that had been arranged by the producer.

'SAVOY TRUFFLE'

It seems that guitarist Eric Clapton's addiction to chocolate inspired Harrison's fourth and final track on the White Album. Based on the contents of a box Mackintosh's Good News chocolates, Harrison managed to get genuine sweet names such as Crème Tangerine, Ginger Sling, Coffee Desert and, of course, Savoy Truffle – an almond based confectionery – into the song, alongside the made-up Cherry Cream and Coconut Fudge.

Harrison admitted that the song was "a funny one written while hanging out with Eric Clapton in the sixties," which was a time when the guitarist ate lots of chocolates – "he couldn't resist them," said Harrison.

"The slow version of 'Revolution' on the album went on and on […] I did a few mixes until I got one I liked"

John Lennon

Left: Ringo Starr joined Cilla Black on her BBC TV show *Cilla* in February 1968.

A

Recording began in Trident on October 3, and continued two days later before the song was completed in Abbey Road on October 11, when six saxophones were recorded in an afternoon session. Producer Martin gave his assistant, Thomas, the job of scoring the song for the brass instruments, something he recalls finding "a real chore."

'CRY BABY CRY'

The whole of July 16 – from 4pm until 9pm – was given over to recording Lennon's song 'Cry Baby Cry', which was when McCartney heard it for the first time. "Because John had divorced Cynthia and gone off with Yoko it meant that I'd hear some of the songs for the first time when he came to the studio."

Written in India, the song parodies a nursery rhyme – 'Sing A Song Sixpence' – and its reference to "cry baby cry/stick a finger in your eye", and the line 'cry baby cry/make your mother buy', which Lennon had seen or heard in an advertisement.

The day The Beatles laid down the first 12 takes of 'Cry Baby Cry' was also the day when their long-time engineer Geoff Emerick quit working with them, explaining later, "I lost interest in the White Album because they were really arguing amongst themselves and swearing at each other. I said to George [Martin] 'Look I've had enough I want to leave. I don't want to know any more.'"

Above: Paul McCartney and John Lennon on the *Tonight Show* in New York with Ed McMahon (l), guest host Joe Garagiola and actress Tellulah Bankhead.

Right: Songwriting partners Paul McCartney and John Lennon got together to announce the launch of Apple Records in May 1968.

However, this explanation isn't the way that Townsend remembers the situation. "He didn't think he had got enough praise for his work on *Sgt Pepper*," says the former head of Abbey Road. "He sent a note to Allan Stagge [the studio manager] saying something like he didn't want to work with The Beatles again because they don't appreciate the work he does for them."

In addition to their usual instruments, The Beatles added organ, piano and harmonium (courtesy of Martin) before finishing the song on July 18. Three months later, when the band were re-mixing 'Cry Baby Cry', journalist Connolly visited Abbey Road. "I was there to interview Yoko Ono about her first album, and I didn't know there had been any rows going on. John was working with George Martin on 'Cry Baby Cry', and Yoko was hanging around and then Paul came in, followed by Linda and her daughter Heather – from then on I never really saw John and Paul together."

That was also the time when Connolly was given a personal recital by a solo Beatle. "Paul came in and took me into a back room where there was a piano and he played 'Let It Be' and 'Lawdy Miss Clawdy'."

'REVOLUTION 9'

This piece of music – it can't really be called a song – was born out of The Beatles' first recording of 'Revolution' (when it had no number) on May 30. By the time they had finished their lengthy session, they had on tape over ten minutes of music, and the last six minutes would be used to create 'Revolution 9'.

Although credited as a Lennon/McCartney composition, it was, in fact, a collaboration of taped sounds collected by Lennon and Ono and, when Lennon returned to the studio on June 10, both Harrison and Starr had flown to America. Working on his own, he compiled more sound effects and, ten days later, by which time McCartney had also left for the USA, Lennon and Ono completed their piece with the help of the now-returned Harrison and Starr.

Explaining his creation, Lennon said, "'Revolution 9' was an unconscious picture of what I actually think will happen when it happens; just like a drawing of a revolution. It was just abstract, loops, people screaming. There are many symbolic things about it but it just happened."

The track was heavily criticized by the music press, with *NME's* Alan Smith deeming it to be "a pretentious piece of codswallop" with the "long, long collection of noises and sounds seemingly dedicated towards expanding sales of Aspro." MM's Alan Walsh was no less scathing, suggesting it was "noisy, boring and meaningless which can only be some private joke for the Beatles' inner circle."

And it seems McCartney was also less than happy with the track as he told Connolly in 1968, "It shouldn't be there, whatever it is, it shouldn't be there." Meanwhile, Lennon, the man who created the piece, said, "I don't know what influence 'Revolution No. 9' had on the teeny-bopper fans, but most of them didn't dig it; so what am I supposed to do?"

'GOOD NIGHT'

Two things about this, the final song on the White Album, stand out – firstly, that it was written by Lennon and, secondly, that it was sung by Starr. It was assumed that, as it was what was described as "a slow, schmaltzy track", it must have been written by McCartney, and most reviewers at the time also assumed it was McCartney's vocal work.

And the man who didn't write it or sing it described 'Good Night' as "the most sentimental little ballad you'll ever hear" and recalled that Lennon, who wrote it as a bedtime song for his son Julian, did sing it to Starr as a guide. "He sang it vey tenderly... I don't think John's version was ever recorded."

Left: Yoko Ono and John Lennon made a guest appearance with David Frost (l) on the *Frost On Saturday* TV show in August 1968.

Recalling his vocal work ago on the song, Starr commented some years later, "I've just heard it for the first time in years and it's not bad at all, although I think I sound very nervous. It was something for me to do."

The Beatles began work on the song on June 28 when it was still listed as 'untitled', and they continued on July 2, taking the total number of takes to 16, but on July 22 they abandoned all their earlier work and started afresh. They moved into the larger Studio One, where an orchestra totalling 26 musicians assembled to add strings, woodwind and brass, while eight singers from the famous Mike Sammes Singers – four men and four women – taped their contribution.

With their new album completed by mid-October, The Beatles, together with Martin but without Harrison, set about organizing the final tracks into an acceptable running order. During the sessions which ran from May to October, they had recorded 32 songs and – after deciding against 'What's the New Mary Jane' and 'Not Guilty' – were left with 30 to go on the four sides of their first double album.

Part-time producer Thomas remembers that the pace of recording changed mid-way through the making of the White Album, particularly when Martin was away. "When George went on holiday the tempo went up like lightening. Suddenly we did something like seven songs in two weeks, whereas before they were doing like one song a week."

And, according to Thomas, that meant more work for Martin. "When George came back we gave him an acetate of all the songs we'd done and he couldn't believe it. I haven't got a clue how or why that happened, maybe some sort of chemistry changed in the room."

The final playlist placed heavier rock songs such as 'Birthday', 'Yer Blues' and 'Helter Skelter' on Side Three, limited each composer to no more than two songs in succession, ensured that each of Harrison's four songs were on separate sides, and put all the "animal" tracks – 'Blackbird', 'Piggies' and 'Rocky Raccoon' – one after another on Side Two.

This was also the time the credits on the album sleeve were confirmed by The Beatles, and Thomas was going to be among those on the list to be thanked, as he recalls. "John and Paul were working out what it should say and

Left: Musician Peter Asher (l) Maureen and Ringo Starr returned to London Heathrow alongside Patti Boyd and George Harrison.

Right: Paul McCartney with his musician father James McCartney who inspired the song 'Honey Pie'.

they started doing these names and John actually said, 'I think Chris's name has to go next to George [Martin].', I witnessed that."

Sadly for Thomas – and everybody else – all these credits were removed when the CD of *The Beatles* was released and, even though he had been mentioned, Thomas was reluctant to share the news. "I never told anyone about it. I thought it would be stupid to say that I had produced The Beatles, I would be setting myself up for a fall. If people asked I would say I worked with them, but I never really spoke about it."

At the end of the recordings, those involved in helping to create the album alongside The Beatles were finally able to hear the end product of their work. "The first time we played 'Back in the U.S.S.R.' back through the speakers it sounded incredible," says Townsend before adding, "Quite a few of the other songs were nondescript but all we were doing was recording songs – one after another. To me it's just an accumulation of songs really."

The Beatles had recorded an astonishing 32 songs in five months, and they were never going to end up with a simple single album, as Martin recalled. "They came in with a whole welter of songs and I was a bit overwhelmed by them, and yet underwhelmed because some of them weren't great."

After dealing with The Beatles using up to three studios at a time to record their individual creations, Martin concluded, "The whole of the album, because there was so much to do, became fragmented" and, when it was over, he was unsure of the end product. "I thought we should probably have made a very, very good single album rather than a double. But they insisted. I think it could have been fantastically good if it had been compressed a bit and condensed."

But, despite the urgings of their long-time producer and advisor, The Beatles dug their heels in, and on November 22, 1968 released their ninth collection of new material – and at the end of the day, almost everybody seemed to be happy with *The Beatles* – the album.

ANOTHER ALBUM, ANOTHER ALBUM COVER

Who do you turn to when the designs for your last album cover broke all the rules in terms of creativity and cost? For The Beatles there was only one solution and, in the wake of the ground-breaking artwork for *Sgt Pepper's Lonely Hearts Club Band*, they once again approached pop-art devotee Robert Fraser.

After introducing the group to *Sgt Pepper* designers Peter Blake and Jann Haworth, gallery owner Fraser had just the man for the next Beatles project – Richard Hamilton, who was acclaimed as one of the the founders of pop art.

After lecturing at Newcastle University – where the future Roxy Music singer Bryan Ferry was his student and describes his teacher as "a great inspiration" – Hamilton, who was a tool draughtsman, developed the concept of pop art through pictures and collages. His vision was that pop art should be "popular, transient, expendable, low-cost, mass-produced, young, witty, sexy, gimmicky, glamorous and Big Business."

Before the album came out, the music press were speculating as to how The Beatles would follow the intricate, colourful and expensive design of *Sgt Pepper*. In October the *NME* reported that the new double album would be packaged "in a cardboard box with a complete set of lyrics."

However, Paul McCartney had other ideas. Having met Hamilton through Fraser, he then called the artist and – after clearing it with his fellow Beatles – invited him to get involved with the group's next album artwork. The first thing they worked on was the creation of a collage of photographs of the four Beatles taken over the years, which would be used as a giveaway poster.

Hamilton explained some years later that, although Paul "wasn't sure about my idea at first", he did come round. "He gave me three tea chests full of photographs to use in the collage."

For student Lynne Timmington, who was specializing in art at Bakewell College in Derbyshire, Hamilton's work had an impact on her, even if she didn't realize it at the time. "Although pop art was not something we studied it had a big influence on a lot of people, and I had a phase of doing montages and collages so maybe it was Hamilton who influenced me without me knowing it."

It seems that the brief Hamilton got from McCartney was to come up with something "as stark a contrast to *Sgt Pepper's* day-glo explosion as possible." His idea was for a plain white sleeve, with the option of a coffee cup stain or even a smudge of apple on it if it was "too clean and empty." He also suggested that the album be called simply *The Beatles* – a title that had never been used before, as McCartney explained. "It had always been *Beatles For Sale*, *Meet The Beatles*, *With The Beatles* but never just *The Beatles*. Richard said that was what we should call it, and everyone agreed."

In an effort to make it less "clean", Hamilton suggested that the group's name be embossed on the sleeve and that each album be given a serial number. His aim was to create the "ironic situation of a numbered edition of something like five million copies", and it was an idea which McCartney bought into as he thought it would be "brilliant for collectors."

For journalist Ray Connolly, the album's title was "daft", and led to the collection being called the White Album almost immediately. "It was not enough to say *The Beatles* although it was fair enough to go the other way after *Sgt Pepper*, but I just thought it wasn't a good title because it was confusing – it could have been a compilation of Beatles things."

While the theory was that something like five million albums would be numbered, it's likely that EMI stopped some way before that, as McCartney explained. "I think EMI only did this on a few thousand and then immediately gave up. Not all 'White' albums have the numbers on them. But it was a good idea."

Right: A limited edition copy of *The Beatles* album, with the serial number 0404532.

"I think it's very much in the artistic mood of the moment"

Mick Brown

Renowned photographer Gered Mankowitz, famous for his work in the sixties with the Rolling Stones, Jimi Hendrix and the Small Faces, was not altogether enamoured by the idea of numbering each album. "I was pretty impressed with the cover, but I think we were all a bit cynical about the numbering and I don't think I missed an image of them."

While he acknowledges that bringing in an established pop artist like Hamilton was "interesting", Mankowitz doesn't think the final artwork changed things very much. "I don't think it set any new standards or became the norm for album covers – and as a photographer, I wanted bands wanting photographs on their covers."

The album package was completed with lyrics printed on the back of the poster, and a set of four individual photographs of The Beatles taken by John Kelly a few months before the album's release. Talking later, Kelly explained his idea. "I said, 'If you have a white cover, you should have some pictures of yourselves inside. Not all together like the "head shot" but individual ones, just straight and simple so the fans have something.' They agreed to do that and I did them at Apple. Paul's picture was taken at Cavendish Avenue."

"The photos inside were iconic and gorgeous. Everything they did was more than it seemed," says Timmington. "Every album cover they

produced was iconic, and for me their covers were almost as important as their music."

For Clifton College student Jonathan Morrish the cover proved one thing. "It was fabulously Beatles – it was them one step ahead of the game. It engaged you as a physical piece of product, and visually it was the deconstruction of everything *Sgt Pepper*."

However, for Roel Kruize and his colleagues at Bovema, EMI's record company in Holland, the arrival of the artwork came as a surprise. "I remember that I looked at the print of the double wallet sleeve and saw all white. I thought 'where is the fucking artwork?' I thought maybe the UK forgot to include the real artwork. My first thought was how I am going to explain this to the dealers, how am I going to advertise this? We were used to colourful sleeves from the flower power era."

By his own admission, Kruize had no idea about "minimalist, avant-garde art", and even had the idea of using the four photographs on

---

Left: John Lennon and Yoko Ono launched 365 'You Are Here' balloons at the opening of his art exhibition at the Robert Fraser gallery.

Above: Robert Fraser, the man who helped create covers for both *Sgt Pepper* and *The Beatles*

the front of the album sleeve to make clear it was a Beatles album. "The next shock was that I saw that the small size of name of The Beatles to be embossed and that the sleeves were individually numbered."

When he then found out that the local Dutch printers could not do either the embossing or the numbering, Kruize was left with only one solution. "I then decided to import finished sleeves from the UK to cope with the initial requirements. Speed was everything to make sure we were on the ball with a Beatles release."

Had the band gone with the idea of calling the album *A Doll's House*, after Henrik Ibsen's 19th-century play, and used a painting by Scottish artist John Byrne, which was under consideration at one point – and was eventually used on *The Beatles Ballads* album – things might have been different. For author and journalist Mick Brown, however, Hamilton's creation was exactly right. "I think it's very much in the artistic mood of the moment – post-psychedelic minimalism."

The man who co-created the ground-breaking *Sgt Pepper* sleeve, Peter Blake, described his design as "highly coloured, very complicated and over-excited" and was truly impressed by Hamilton's work on the follow-up release. "A plain white cover which was brilliant and a total contrast," he said before adding, "I think our two sleeves work in conjunction."

Although it would be another six years before he hit the charts with Cockney Rebel, Steve Harley was a teenage fan of both the music and the creativity of The Beatles, and suggests that there might have been a message behind Hamilton's cover artwork. "Wasn't it their way of saying this isn't *Sgt Pepper*, where every square inch was covered in art and the next one comes out and there's nothing?"

And Harley is happy to give the credit to McCartney. "I get the impression that Paul said we should go this way, it looks like a Paul idea. It's very clever marketing, everyone was looking

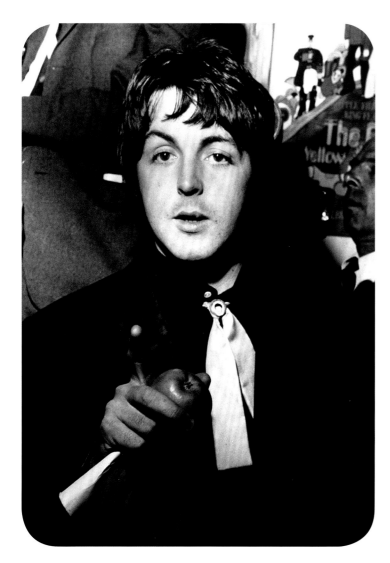

Left: Pop art 'guru' Richard Hamilton who designed the artwork for the White Album – and got paid £200.

Above: Paul McCartney finds a subtle way of promoting The Beatles' Apple empire.

Right: John Lennon and Yoko Ono at the June 1968 premiere of his play *In His Own Write* at the Old Vic theatre in London.

for the stamp – the limited edition number." As if to prove his point, he says, "I've got a nice low number which I bought very early on from my local record shop."

The lowest numbers were, in fact, grabbed, understandably, by The Beatles themselves, with McCartney recalling that John Lennon got 000001 "because he shouted loudest." If he did get the first copy, he obviously didn't keep it, as it was Ringo Starr who put it up for auction in America in December 2015. He claimed he got the coveted British number-000001 album "because I'm lovely", and it fetched a world-record price of $790,000, while the 000005 copy sold for £19,000 in 2008.

But while the artwork he created became highly desirable and extremely expensive, Hamilton, who died in 2011, recalled that, like Blake before him, he was only paid around £200 for his efforts. "I thought that was a bit mean. I was surprised how little we got."

RECEPTION

By 1968 The Beatles were well established as the biggest band in the world. Their record sales were calculated in the hundreds of millions, and they had more No. 1 hits than any of their rivals but, with *The Beatles*, they showed that they could still surprise people.

At precisely the same time as The Beatles prepared to launch their new album into the hands of hungry fans and anxious critics alike, a young man was beginning his career at Abbey Road Studios.

Alan Parsons, who would go on to produce No. 1 records for Pilot and Cockney Rebel, was just 19 when he began working in what was undoubtedly the most famous studio in the world. "I was there for the final two weeks when The Beatles were making the White Album, and I wandered the corridors trying to get a glimpse of a Beatle but I never saw one."

But what the man who created the multi-million selling *Alan Parson Project* albums did come across was something that the group he didn't see had actually made. "I was working on my first studio session in Studio Three, with a band called The Gods, when we came across a tape that was just lying around – there was no security back then. We stuck it on, and it was 'Back in the U.S.S.R.'"

The band, featuring future Uriah Heep keyboard player Ken Hensley, producer David Paramor and Parsons, were all suitably impressed with their sneak preview. "It sounded finished to me, it was utterly brilliant and we all looked at each other and thought 'it makes you want to give up.'. It was the standout track on the album."

In the weeks between The Beatles' final recording session for the White Album – on October 14 – and the album's release in November, the group went through Lennon & Ono's court case on drug charges, Cynthia Lennon's successful divorce petition, the Starr family moving house, Harrison guesting on a US-television comedy show, and Ono suffering a miscarriage the day before the album came out.

The Beatles, or the White Album, as it would be forever called, finally came out amid stories that it contained 30 songs simply because the group were anxious to fulfil their 1967 nine-year deal with EMI as quickly as possible. There was a clause in the contract negotiated by Brian Epstein which said that the group would only record for four years, and make no more than 70 sides during the nine years up to 1976.

Perhaps this contractual arrangement also explained the absence of any singles from the album, although Ken Townsend explains, "The Beatles had their principles. They were adamant that there would be no singles on the album. I heard them say that it was 'cheating the public' if you did that."

Ahead of the release, stories began to appear in the music press that the group would be spending £16,000 on TV adverts to promote the album. The plan, according to the *NME*, was for the commercials to be aired across all ITV stations on Sunday, November 17 and either Paul McCartney or Ringo Starr would feature as the voice-over.

A week later came another news report ,which told readers that the plan had been dropped because, according to somebody at Apple, the "expense involved was too great." So it was left to full-page newspaper advertisements to let everyone know that *The Beatles* was in the shops.

Following the style of the album-sleeve design, the adverts were completely white with the words THE BEATLES in white capital letters with black edging and the text "Special Double Album – Released November 22". While the Apple logo was featured alongside EMI's sign, the catalogue numbers – PMC 7067-8 (M) and PCS 7067-8 (S) – confirmed it was an EMI release.

Meanwhile, over in the Netherlands, the staff at Bovema were about to get their first listen to the brand new music from The Beatles, as Roel Kruize recalls. "We got the test pressing from the factory and put on the first album and heard 'Back in the U.S.S.R.' We were over the moon, great track for a single, that's what we thought."

Then those assembled in the meeting at the company's headquarters in Haarlem listened some more. "We were expecting more tracks like this, but while listening to the rest of the tracks we were getting quite confused because of the variety of styles, songs and sounds on the album," says Kruize, who adds, "I was thinking 'anyway, hey this is a Beatles album, it's going to be great saleswise.'"

However, Kruize, who was label manager for Beatles' releases in the Netherlands, had some doubts. "My initial 'artistic' feeling was that this was not a cohesive album at all. Yet there were enough tracks that I really liked – 'Ob-La-Di, Ob-La-Da', 'Blackbird' and 'While My Guitar Gentle Weeps' – and that stood out for me. Others were OK."

But, like so many others, he "really hated Revolution 9" and was disappointed with the Ringo tracks. "Actually I felt it was not a Beatles album anymore, but style exercises for solo albums and careers to come. Of course I knew that since Yoko's arrival, there was not much harmony anymore between the key songwriters. Later in the development of the album, and after more listenings, I found other tracks that were also very good. It was all very daring at the time, and only the Beatles could afford to do this."

Beatles engineer Geoff Emerick, who ended his relationship with The Beatles during the making of the album but returned in April 1969, recalls how the album was received by the media. "The White Album was released to mixed reviews. Some people consider it their favourite Beatles

Above: John Lennon and Yoko Ono were almost inseparable during the six months spent recording the White Album in Abbey Road.

A

album." He then adds his own assessment. "Personally I think it's their least inspired effort, and I find it difficult to listen to. There was little finesse; the group seemed to be simply trying to get something out of their system."

Although he wasn't handed a copy of the album at end of his shift with The Beatles, Chris Thomas, who was in charge on 13 Beatles' sessions over an 18-day period, did eventually get one. "I didn't get a copy for quite a few months and I had to ask George Martin if I could have one – and my number is something like 485,000." And the occasional producer also admits that listening to records you've worked on is not always easy. "It's like *Alice Through The Looking Glass* – you listen to it in a totally different way, there's no mystery so I cannot judge it. But The Beatles were breaking ground with a double album."

Music author and former editor of *Melody Maker* Ray Coleman was another who saw the White Album as a clear indication that things were changing. "Here was the first real proof that the 'fab four' weren't the happy beat quartet of fond memory, and there was a clear distinction between Lennon and McCartney songs."

Although the official release date was November 22, it's clear that the major music papers of the day were given advance copies of the album for review, as both *MM* and *NME* printed reviews in their November 9 issues. *MM*'s Alan Walsh, a Liverpudlian who was this author's editor in 1969 on the music trade paper *Music Business Weekly*, wrote, "The album illustrates that the four members can each have their own direction under the artistic umbrella of the Beatles; pulling in different directions but never catapulting into anarchy."

At the same time, *NME*'s Alan Smith proclaimed that the album was "one of the most significant landmarks in their recording career since 'Love Me Do' [...] presenting the sheer good, bad and ugly of their work to late October 1968." He went on to say, "*The Beatles* offers so many brilliant Lennon-McCartney future standards, and so much inventiveness from all of them, that it has been well worth waiting for."

Left: Writer and critic Ray Connolly (left), pictured with David Essex, was among the journalists who praised The Beatles' latest work.

The music critics on Britain's national newspapers were split, with the *Observer*'s Tony Palmer commenting that "if there is still any doubt that Lennon and McCartney are the greatest songwriters since Schubert, [the album] should surely see the last vestiges of cultural snobbery and bourgeois prejudice swept away in a deluge of joyful music-making."

Derek Jewell in the *The Sunday Times* was just as effusive, hailing it as "the best thing in pop since *Sgt Pepper*" before adding, "Musically there is beauty, horror, surprise, chaos, order. And that is the world; and that is what The Beatles are on about." His colleague on *The Times*, William Mann, suggested that, while Lennon and McCartney had "ceased to progress as songwriters", the album was "The most important musical event of the year."

Ray Connolly in the *London Evening Standard* concluded, "The Beatles are still a really vibrant and 'together' beat group, as well as being the best songwriters of their generation." Barry Miles was owner of the Indica Gallery and at the heart of London's art scene in the mid-sixties, and he also co-founded the *International Times*, which carried his review of the White Album in November 1968. "Well the new Beatles album's here with 30 catchy little numbers for you to whistle on your way to work, glide round the Mecca to, swoon in your bed-sit, dance to at the hoe-down, play down on the farm, revive the jive, stomp to at your local rock palace, or sing on the way to Grosvenor Square."

Critics in America were even more divided

in their opinion, with Nik Cohn writing in the *New York Times* that the album was "boring beyond belief" and describing half of the songs as "profound mediocrities." In the same newspaper, Richard Goldstein told readers that the album was "a major success" and "far more imaginative than *Sgt Pepper*."

And while *Time* magazine declared that the album showed the band's "best abilities and worst tendencies" while lacking a "sense of taste and purpose", US music trade magazine *Billboard* described *The Beatles* as their "most ambitious, most impressive effort to date."

A year on from its launch, *Rolling Stone* magazine was able to review a Beatles album made up of brand-new tracks for the first time, and founder and editor Jann Wenner concluded, "Whatever else it is or isn't, it is the best album they have ever released, and only The Beatles are capable of making a better one. You are either hip or you ain't. In short it is the new Beatles record and it fulfils all our expectations of it."

While American Christian evangelist David Noebel was pronouncing that the lyrics of 'Back in the U.S.S.R.' were further proof of The Beatles' compliance in a Communist plot to brainwash the youth of America, the group's newest release was storming the best-seller charts all over the world.

But Radio 1 disc jockey Keith Skues said the new Beatles double album – with no singles – wasn't able to be featured in his shows. "I was presenting programmes such as *Saturday Club, What's New* and *Family Choice,* and no tracks from the album were selected for any of my shows," he explained. And the man who moved to the BBC from pirate station Radio Caroline in 1967 added, "I did mention it to my producer at *Saturday Club,* but he firmly told me that he selected the music."

With or without radio airplay, the album debuted at No. 1 in the UK on December 7, and remained there for seven weeks until *Best of The Seekers*, from Australian quartet The Seekers, took over the top spot on January 25, 1969 – the first time an Australian act had topped any UK chart. However, after just one week *The Beatles* was back at the top for an eighth and final week.

Dick James, the head of Northern Songs, the publishers of Lennon/McCartney songs, announced to the world that sales of the new album were "phenomenal", and a front-page story in *MM* – under the headline "£1 Million For Beatles New LP" – reported that advance orders had passed the £1 million mark and EMI had shipped 100,000 copies into UK shops on the day of release.

However, the first Beatles double album provided EMI with a whole new set of problems: as there were two records to go in each cover, they had to be hand-sleeved, as opposed to the usual automatic process, and only twenty double albums could be packed in each carton, which weighed a hefty 30lbs (13.6kgs), while the photographs were delivered separately to retailers to be inserted

Within a week *The Beatles* was at No. 1 in Australia, Canada, France, Norway and West Germany, while in America Capitol Records sold over 3 million copies into record stores within four days. Consequently, on December 14 it debuted at No. 11, jumped to No. 2 the following week, and topped the US album chart on December 28 – and stayed there for nine weeks, spending a total of 155 weeks on the *Billboard* 200 chart.

In the midst of all this frantic chart activity, fans were airing their views in letters to the music press. Peter Lawrence, an Englishman living in California, wrote to *NME* to say, "The new Beatles LP is the greatest thing to come out of a recording studio in recent years!"

Meanwhile, D Beasley in Birmingham asked, "Why have The Beatles spoilt such a masterpiece with the atrocity they call 'Revolution 9'?", and Dave Robinson from Manchester declared, "How Lennon McCartney could have allowed the rubbish ['Revolution 9'] to ruin such a brilliantly inventive album is beyond my comprehension."

MM also received correspondence from their readers, with Munro Teale from Southport stating, "Today I am selling my eight Beatles LPs. Gone are the smiling faces delivering good tunes with melodic backing. Now we have to listen to monotonous, gimmick-ridden sensational trash."

For Roxy Music guitarist Phil Manzanera, 1968 marked his eighth year in Britain after leaving Venezuela, and in January of that year, courtesy of his brother, he met up with Dave Gilmour and Robert Wyatt. "Still at school and I had met two people from two of the coolest bands in London... Pink Floyd and Soft Machine."

Fired by an ambition to be a musician, Manzanera, in his own words, was "obsessed with rock 'n' roll and especially The Beatles" and saw the release of a new album as "momentous". He had devoured all the fab four's earlier albums, but their 1968 offering was not as easy to digest. "However when it came out, as it was a double, it was confusing and difficult to grasp initially as there was so much of it. All the other albums were more focused and shorter, and this really was exploratory and long."

Listening to the album, Manzanera, who would join Roxy Music in 1972, gradually focused on the individual tracks. "I was drawn first to 'While My Guitar Gently Weeps' being a guitarist and hearing rumours that 'God', Eric Clapton, was on it. Slowly other gems began to reveal themselves but it was uneven. I particularly liked 'Back in the U.S.S.R.', 'Dear Prudence', 'Happiness Is a Warm Gun' and 'Blackbird'."

However, music was changing, and the likes of Soft Machine, Pink Floyd, Cream, Velvet Underground, King Crimson, Grateful Dead and the Mothers of Invention were all making an impression on Manzanera who admits, "The accumulation of great albums began to distract me away, and open my mind away from the fab four."

A couple of other people with particularly close links to the music business in 1968 when *The Beatles* came out were photographer Gered Mankowitz and journalist Connolly, who recalls that what he heard back then was "a mishmash", which "would have made one great album – there would have been 14 great tracks."

He also confirms what he heard from the band members. "John said it was Paul with a backing group, and Paul said it was John and a backing group, but it was a backing group that knew each other well – it wasn't just any backing group."

For Mankowitz, who would later photograph the likes of Kate Bush, Bing Crosby and the Eurythmics, the album showed that the avant-garde music of people like Frank Zappa and Captain Beefheart was having a big influence on everybody. "The Beatles were evolving – in fact everybody was evolving very rapidly in this rather focused and concentrated collapse of the sixties. The versatility of *The Beatles* was very attractive – they mixed it all up and had fun tracks."

Two musicians – one already a hit-maker and the other yet to make his mark – were also keen listeners to the new Beatles album when it came out. Junior Campbell's group Marmalade had charted twice in 1968 before 'Ob-La-Di, Ob-La-Da' came their way from the White Album. "I bought it – and still have it – but I thought it was pretty unremarkable considering what they had done before. It seemed pretty fractious to me in terms of songwriting, and the cracks were beginning to appear, but at the time we were all too busy doing our thing for critical analysis."

Steve Harley and his band Cockney Rebel didn't debut on the UK charts until 1974, but the aspiring musician was already an ardent Beatles fan in the sixties. "Beatles albums are a major part of my life and always will be, but the White Album is not one of them. It was too long and you had to get through a lot of padding to get to the good stuff."

Having bought a copy of the album, Harley, who was working as a journalist in 1968, was disappointed. "When the album ended after something like two hours we weren't impressed with it. It represented a career on its down slope." Another let-down was the absence of the group's two hit singles from the album. "The best two tracks from this year – 'Lady Madonna' and 'Hey Jude' – were put out as singles and not on the album – and they needed them on this

album. They were two better songs than almost anything on the album."

While renowned guitarist, singer and songwriter Richard Thompson, who left Fairport Convention to perform with his wife Linda, considered *Sgt Pepper* to be "overrated", he was even less impressed with the White Album. "It doesn't sound like a band anymore. It's individuals doing their own thing, although there are good bits here and there."

Most of the people who bought the White Album in 1968 were music fans in their late teens or early twenties, and journalist Mick Brown, born in 1950, was among them. "It was very much a hit-and-miss album, but there was a huge burden of expectation following *Sgt Pepper* and maybe they felt that. Some of the songs are throwaway riffs that have been developed into songs, but they are not songs in a completed or evolved sense. But they could do anything because they were The Beatles."

Considering the music that he first heard in 1968, Brown says, "As a social document of the time this was the Beatles' most important record – a reflection of where they were and where they were at."

Future producer and musician Alan Parsons recalls that he got his copy through EMI's in-house sales system. "I bought it through staff sales. You filled in a requisition form which went to the Hayes factory, and you'd get the album at a discount. It never struck me at the time as being an album that was made during any sort of discord – it was The Beatles and there were so many different styles on the album."

Liz Woodcraft was in her first term at university in the autumn of 1968 and, although she wasn't a Beatles fan, it was hard not to be affected by their music. "I heard the White Album because up the road from me in Birmingham were a load of male students and everybody there was sitting round smoking dope and listening to it. I just thought it was the most boring thing in the world, but I still knew all the words and could sing along to it."

Another student was 19 year-old Lynne Timmington but she didn't have a record player in her room at teacher training college in Bakewell, Derbyshire. "I was absolutely hooked on The Beatles – they were special – and we played the album at weekends when I came home," she recalls, and her boyfriend (now husband) Tony was encouraging her. "He was working on a cruise liner and he wrote to me about 'While My Guitar Gently Weeps', saying it was fabulous and that he was playing it over and over."

Respected music writer, author and publisher David Hepworth was just 18 years old when he bought *The Beatles*. "I bought every Beatles record and I took the poster out of this one and put it on my bedroom wall – I think it had some nakedness in it somewhere, which made it slightly controversial in my mother's eyes."

While the man who launched *Q*, *Mojo* and *The Word* magazines was not a fan of 'Revolution 9' – "played it once and never again" – he did get through the rest of the album. "One of the things that made the Beatles so great was their tendency to let their enthusiasm get the better of them, and that's nowhere more the case than with the White Album.

"The avant garde stuff is more unlistenable, the rockers are more raucous, the sentimental ones are more sugary, the wacky stuff is wackier than anywhere else. I suspect this was the case because it was basically three solo albums."

Mark Rye became head of EMI's Harvest label in the mid-seventies, but he was just 17 when he got to hear the White Album – in his hospital bed. "I was lying in a hospital bed after breaking my leg playing hockey. I asked my mum to go and buy me a copy, and she brought [it] into the hospital along with a record player."

After that, life got even better for Rye when a friend came off his scooter and was admitted to the same hospital. "They put the two of us on a side ward where we could be youths and play music. All the young nurses popped in to listen to the White Album which we very nearly wore out – and we knew every track in great detail. For us it was essential listening."

Future head of PR for CBS Records and Sony Music in the UK, Jonathan Morrish, was in his last term at Clifton College when the White Album came out. "I do remember that we had an in-house tutor who was probably in his mid-twenties, and he went out and got it. Then a bunch of us went into his room late at night and listened to it – that was when I first heard it."

And he was impressed with what he heard. "I don't think it's an indifferent double album and we should never forget how brilliantly sequenced it is – it is absolute genius. For me it is the album when The Beatles find freedom as individuals, expressing themselves as songwriters – and they were without Brian Epstein, which was important."

Morrish was also impressed with the different songwriting styles adopted by the group. "They were still writing singles because they could still write short stories at the same time as creating a novel, and they could afford not to put the short stories [singles] on the album. It shows how the sum of the parts is greater than the whole."

Twenty-one-year-old Alan Thompson was living in Chelmsford in 1968 and his first memory of the White Album is that he didn't buy a copy. "I wasn't a great Beatles fan and was more into the Stones and R&B," he recalls. However, things changed in 1968 at the family Christmas in Bournemouth, where his aunt had a boarding house.

"There were so many people staying there that I was put out to a friend's boarding house, and there I met an Australian girl who had got the album. I listened to it on her Dansette record player and enjoyed it. Early on the Beatles were a very polished sort of pop act, but this had a mysticism and excitement about it, and it was apparent that they were now doing exactly what they wanted to do on their records."

While everybody else was passing an opinion on their new release, The Beatles also gave thought to what they had created during the half-year spent in and out of the studio. While Starr simply said that the album "had some

BEATLES HAND OUT BOUTIQUE CLOTHES FREE

FRANKLIN

"Ringo got a bit carried away, officer.."

great music", McCartney announced that, while it was "a very good album", it wasn't "a pleasant one to make", before going on to explain, "I don't remember the reaction. I can't ever remember scouring the charts to see what number it had come in at. If your mates liked it, the boutiques played it and it was played wherever you went – that was a sign of success."

As far as Harrison was concerned, The Beatles began work on the album during a "period that started as a bit negative… it was a bit difficult" but they survived. "We finally got through the album and everybody was pleased because the tracks were good."

Irrespective of the opinions of fans and critics – and the band – the end of 1968 saw the album officially titled *The Beatles* sitting at No. 1 in the charts in both the UK and US, where they had also begun the year in the top spot with

Magical Mystery Tour. Over the following year, sales continued and, by the end of the decade, the White Album sat at No. 3 in the list of the UK's best-selling albums of the sixties – behind *Sgt Pepper* and *The Sound of Music*.

However, despite the success of their album, Lennon did not hold back when asked about the White Album. In a 1971 interview, which was eventually published in *Penthouse* magazine in 1984, he explained, "He [Paul] wanted it to be more a group thing, which really means more Paul. So he never liked that album and I always preferred it to all the other albums including *Sgt Pepper*. The *Pepper* myth is bigger, but the music on the White album is far superior."

Above: Stanley Franklin's cartoon at the time of the closure of the Apple boutique.

IT WAS FIFTY
YEARS AGO TODAY

Half a century after getting an unauthorized sneak preview of a track from *The Beatles*, Alan Parsons reflects on the music the group made back in 1968. "It was a big album with a lot of songs to choose from, and some are my absolute favourites and some are my least favourites."

Adding that he would still play the White Album for pleasure – "but probably not all of it" – Parsons, who worked as engineer on The Beatles' Savile Row roof-top sessions and on their final *Abbey Road* album in 1969, states, "The whole Beatles experience had a huge influence on what I went on to do in the studio."

In 2011 journalist Jon Dennis wrote in *The Guardian* that the White Album was his favourite album, although he didn't hear it until ten years after it had been released. He explained that, in the late seventies, "just as pop music was moving out from the shadow of the sixties and getting interesting again," he and his best friend discovered The Beatles.

It was on Christmas Day 1978 when Dennis first heard the record and he wrote that "nothing had really prepared us for the White Album." In his article, he wrote of "the blank sleeve", which "gave nothing away", and described the songs on the album as being "in conflict rather than harmony", and defended the idea of it being a double set. "I disagree with the suggestion that the White Album should have been a single album. Its flaws make it more interesting. And its sprawl, endless variety, and the Beatles' adventures into the subconscious, makes it unknowable."

On the tenth anniversary of the release of *The Beatles*, EMI reissued the two albums as a limited-edition white vinyl set and, three years later, in 1981, Mobile Fidelity Sound put out a half-speed master variation using the original master recording and pressed each album on top-quality virgin vinyl.

A year ahead of the White Album's 20th-birthday celebration in 1988, EMI, who were late-comers to the new world of compact discs, issued the double album as a double CD with Sides One and Two of the album on Disc 1 and Sides Three and Four on Disc 2. Sales of the new format took the album into the CD charts, newly compiled in the UK and US the same year.

In the UK, *The Beatles* CD reached No. 1 in early September before slipping to No. 9 while, in America, the CD version entered at No. 29 on September 12 and a week later rose to No. 4, and finally took the top spot on September 19 before being replaced by Michael Jackson's album *Bad*. The CD release also boosted sales of the vinyl album, which hit the top twenty in Britain, reached No. 4 in Japan, but peaked at No. 23 in the Netherlands and a lowly No. 87 in the US.

The collected data concerning the White Album proves that, while it might not be the best-selling Beatles album, it has done pretty well over the 50 years since its release. In the list of all-time best-selling albums – which is headed up by Jackson's *Thriller* at 66 million – *The Beatles* doesn't figure in the top twenty with sales of around 9.5 million but, as a double album, it can be (and often is) credited with sales of 19 million. However, it still comes in as the fourth best-selling Beatles album of all time behind *1* (23 million), *Abbey Road* (14.4 million) and *Sgt Pepper's Lonely Hearts Club Band* (13.1 million).

The Recording Industry Association of America (RIAA) has recognized the status of *The Beatles* as a double album, and certified it as 19 times platinum for sales of 19 million while, in the UK, where certified sales awards weren't introduced until 1973, it is recognized as a platinum album with sales of 300,000. Meanwhile, Canada has awarded the album eight platinum discs (600,000) and it has gone double platinum in Australia (140,000) and New Zealand (30,000).

Renowned Beatles' historian Ken Womack was a 12-year-old child living in America when he first came across *The Beatles*. "I first encountered the LP as a pre-teen in 1978. At the time, I had been slowly consuming The Beatles' music, album by album, and by the advent of my birthday that January, the White Album made its first appearance on my turntable, courtesy of my Aunt Molly."

After enjoying his 12th-birthday celebrations, it was time for Womack to listen to his latest present. "I secreted myself upstairs to listen to the strange album with its blank-white cover for the very first time. I will never forget playing Side One and realizing, as 'Back in the U.S.S.R.' tumbled into 'Dear Prudence', that this LP was something altogether different. And by the time that 'Glass Onion' was cued up, any lingering doubts were all but extinguished.

"As the surreal song raced to an end, there they were – those lyrics – as stark as day 'Trying to make a dovetail joint,'" says Womack before adding, "'Good God,' I thought to myself. 'I'll surely be listening to this album through my headphones from now on.' If Aunt Molly only knew what she'd just laid at my feet."

Even after his father, a hotshot carpenter in his own right, explained the dovetail joint's place in fine furniture construction, Womack's thoughts went back in time. "Whenever I hear that line – even years later – I revisit that initial, tiny frisson of fear as something unexplainable, something contraband entered my adolescent world for the very first time."

In the years since the release of *The Beatles/White Album*, critics have returned to the album to re-assess its importance, its relevance and the quality of the music. *Q* magazine, first published in October 1986, suggested "Falling apart, they [The Beatles] still made music that eclipsed most other groups" while *Mojo*, founded in 1993, said, "Whatever the traumas, the White Album became simply breathtaking in its diversity – lush ballads, heavy metal, country, reggae, whimsy, avant garde collage and throwaway pop tunes all find a comfortable home – and most of it is wonderful."

Rolling Stone magazine's 2004 Album Guide described the songs on the album as ranging from "the sturdiest tunes since *Revolver* to self-indulgent fillers", and, in the same magazine's

Right: Alan Parsons began his career at Abbey Road where he worked with The Beatles before founding the Alan Parsons Project.

2003 List of the Top 200 Albums of all-time, *The Beatles* featured at No. 10, a position it still held in a 2012 update – behind a Beatles One, Two and Three thanks to *Sgt Pepper*, *Revolver* and *Rubber Soul*.

The Guinness Rockopedia, published thirty years after the album's release, said, "The record found all four members on superb form although it is often considered more the work of solo artists than true collaborators" and, ten years later, *L'Osservatore Romano*, the esteemed Vatican newspaper, was moved to add that the album "remains a type of magical musical anthology: 30 songs you can go through and listen to at will."

The White Album's listing in *1001 Albums You Must Hear Before You Die*, published in 2005, said, "Amid band squabbling The Beatles produced *The Beatles*, an epic masterpiece that equals *Sgt Pepper*" while Martin Strong's' 2004 *Great Rock Discography* described the album as "A sprawling double set recorded in an environment of tension and breakdown of inter-band communications. Yet it contained some of the Beatles finest songs."

By the time the world welcomed the new millennium in 2000, there were just three tracks on *The Beatles* album which had not been covered by anybody at all, anywhere. They were, not surprisingly perhaps, 'Wild Honey Pie' and 'Revolution 9' plus 'Revolution 1', although the version on the B-side of 'Hey Jude', entitled simply 'Revolution', could claim covers by Billy Bragg, the Thompson Twins and Mike and The Mechanics.

Among the array of cover versions of other songs from the White Album are 'Martha My Dear' by Slade; 'Good Night' by ex-Monkee Mickey Dolenz, Ella Fitzgerald's 'Savoy Truffle', 'Piggies' by Chumbawamba's Danbert Bacon, and 'Sexy Sadie' by Paul Weller.

Writing in 2009, the *Daily Telegraph's* music writer Neil McCormick suggested that *The Beatles* was "one of the greatest albums ever made" while Hunter Davies, author of the first and only authorized biography of The Beatles – published six months before the White Album came out – gave his opinion in 2016. Awarding the album eight 'mop-tops' (his version of a star rating), he wrote, "They had ceased to be each other's friends and the atmosphere during much of the studio work was becoming pretty much fragile and fraught. But really, as far as

Above: Legendary jazz singer Ella Fitzgerald was one of many artists to record their own take on tracks from the White Album.

Right: John Lennon (l) and Paul McCartney (r) brave the elements alongside Ringo Starr and George Harrison at Wapping Pier on the River Thames during their 'Mad Day Out' photo session.

the tracks on the album went, it didn't show."

While others focused their critic's ears on the music made by The Beatles on their 1968 double album, a gallery in New York set up an "installation" piece in 2013. The Recess Gallery in the city's SoHo district showed a piece by artist Rutherford Chang which featured a record store displaying only original numbered pressings of the album – there were 693 of them from Chang's collection of over 1,900 original 1968 albums. It was accompanied by a recording of 100 copies of the album electronically overlaid to create one 96-minute double LP.

Fifty years on from its original release, all the talk is about a possible celebratory remixed box set including out-takes and alternate versions of songs from *The Beatles* album; and despite producer Giles Martin, George's son and the man who re-mixed the 2017 *Sgt Pepper* box set, denying any involvement – "I'm not working on it" – the rumour mill continues to spin.

Finally, if you were one of the millions who shelled out the princely sum of £3.14s, .10d (£3.72p) or thereabouts from your pocket money, weekly allowance or wage packet and managed to get hold of an early numbered copy of *The Beatles* (ideally between 1 and 100), it might be some consolation to know that it could bring you between £4,000 ($5,500) and £10,000 ($14,000) today. On the other hand, if you wanted to buy a second-hand copy of the album – in good condition – you would expect to pay anywhere between £24 ($33) and £30 ($41).

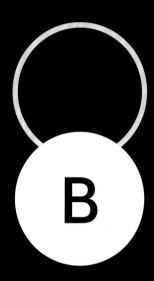

B-Side

1967
THE YEAR WHEN THE WORLD CHANGED

If 1966 was London's time in the spotlight as the capital city setting new trends in music, fashion, sex and drugs, 1967 saw a growing revolutionary awareness of politics, protest, psychedelia and festivals emerge from across the Atlantic.

America was still involved in an on-going war in Vietnam, and increasing racial tension brought people out onto the streets across the USA, at the same time that psychedelic pop and "flower power" was spreading from the West Coast.

But despite the new wave of liberalism and creative freedom, some of America's establishment stood their ground – as the Rolling Stones discovered. Their performance on the *Ed Sullivan Show* to perform 'Let's Spend The Night Together' required them to change the lyrics to "let's spend some time together." However, it seems Mick Jagger settled for a lengthy "mmmmmmmm" instead, and the band were never invited back on to the show. And in England the Stones caused further furore, when they refused to join the traditional revolving stage at the end of the *Sunday Night at the London Palladium* TV show.

At the same time the "space race" was under way, but the USA's programme suffered a major tragedy when astronauts Roger Chafee, Virgil Grissom and Ed White died in a fire in *Apollo 1* at Cape Canaveral; then three months later, in April, U.S.S.R. cosmonaut Vladimir Komarov also perished when his spaceship crash-landed.

February opened with EMI telling the world that The Beatles' world sales had reached a staggering 180 million in the four-plus years since they released their debut single. Meanwhile, arch rivals the Stones were in trouble with the police after they raided Keith Richards' home in Chichester, Sussex, and served summonses under the Dangerous Drugs Act to Richards and Mick Jagger.

A new satirical underground magazine appeared on British news stands as *Oz* arrived from Australia, with a cover price of 2s .6d (12.5p) and, soon after, Jimi Hendrix released 'Purple Haze', which *MM* decided was "difficult to assess." The same paper declared that Pink Floyd's debut single, 'Arnold Layne', represented "a new form of pop music."

In April, after 10 years of trying, Britain finally won the Eurovision Song Contest when Sandie Shaw triumphed in Vienna with 'Puppet on a String', and reigning football world champions England lost to Scotland at Wembley, ending an unbeaten run of 19 games.

While America had deployed over 400,000 troops to Vietnam, two major anti-war protests in New York and San Francisco brought over 300,000 people out on the streets. At the other end of the spectrum, psychedelia moved from the US West Coast to London's Alexandra Palace for the '14 Hour Technicolor Dream, where Pink Floyd, Soft Machine and Alex Harvey played to 7,000 people and raised money for the cash-strapped *International Times* counterculture magazine.

Flower power took over the pop charts in May, when Scott Mackenzie's 'San Francisco (Be Sure To Wear Flowers in Your Hair)' peaked at No. 3 in the US but topped the charts in Britain, Germany, Belgium and Denmark, selling over seven million copies. Finally, six years after being turned down, Britain – along with Ireland, Denmark and Norway – were allowed to re-apply for membership of the European Economic Community (EEC).

The end of May saw two major "firsts" for Britain as Scotland's Celtic became the first British soccer team to win the European Cup – beating Inter Milan 2-1 – and Francis Chichester completed the first single-handed round-the-world yacht trip, sailing over 28,000 miles in 226 days.

America experienced more anti-war protests as 100,000 people took to the streets in New York when the US Government increased bombing raids over Vietnam, and 10,000 protesters

"It was a beginning of change, but not exactly as we had hoped"

Liz Woodcraft

occupied Century Plaza in Los Angeles. Israel declared their own war in the Middle East and launched raids on Syria, Jordan, Iraq and Egypt before agreeing to a cease-fire and ending the so-called Six-Day War. As a result, Egypt blocked the Suez Canal, and it remained closed to shipping for eight years.

Britain's Decca Records celebrated their fastest-ever selling single, when Procol Harum's chart-topper 'A Whiter Shade of Pale' passed the 600,000 mark.

Running from June 16–18, the world's first major pop festival took place in Monterey, California, with The Who, Jimi Hendrix, the Byrds, Grateful Dead, Otis Redding and the Mamas and the Papas. More than 50,000 people attended the event, which had been organized by a foundation that included John Phillips, Paul McCartney, Mick Jagger, Brian Wilson and Smokey Robinson. At the same time, in Switzerland, the first ever Montreux Jazz Festival was held and featured Miles Davis, Bill Evans, Nina Simone and Ella Fitzgerald.

At the end of June, world heavyweight boxing champion Muhammed Ali, who had been indicted for refusing to be drafted into the US Army to fight in Vietnam, was sent to prison for five years and fined $10,000. His jail sentence was quashed on appeal, but he was still stripped of his boxing title and banned from fighting for three years.

Following the police raid in February, Rolling Stones Jagger and Richards appeared in court in June on drug charges and were each sentenced to jail – Jagger got three months, while Richards was given a year – and they spent the night in prison before being allowed out on bail. July began with a major campaign against the prison terms, which involved *The Times*, *Sunday Express* and *London Evening News*. The result was that Richards had his

Left: World boxing champion Muhammed Ali faces the press during a break in his trial in Houston, Texas on a charge of draft dodging.

"Young people were very disenchanted with Labour for killing off pirate radio"

Alan Thompson

conviction quashed, and Jagger's sentence was reduced to a conditional discharge.

All this coincided with the British Parliament taking the momentous step to legalize sexual intercourse between consenting men over the age of 21, and also imposing a 70 mph speed limit on Britain's roads.

Across the Atlantic, America experienced a series of major race riots in Newark, Detroit and Minneapolis, which saw 69 people killed and damage to property totalling $4 million.

Britain continued its affair with the hippie movement as Alexandra Palace hosted a "Love-In Festival" with Eric Burdon and Brian Auger topping the bill. It ran from 9pm through to 9am the next morning, and tickets cost £1.

In August folk singer Joan Baez, a long-time supporter of the US anti-Vietnam war movement, confronted the Daughters of the American Revolution, who objected to her protesting and banned her from performing in Washington DC's Constitution Hall. She declared that they had "a different idea of freedom from what I have."

Searching for their own brand of peaceful awareness, The Beatles – along with wives and girlfriends, plus Mick Jagger and Marianne Faithfull – travelled to Bangor in North Wales to attend a seminar held by the Maharishi Mahesh Yogi and, while there, received the news that their long-time manager Brian Epstein had died.

Britain's Labour Government took action against the pirate radio ships moored around the coast when, on August 14, they introduced the Marines Offences Act, which claimed that "legal" radio stations across Europe had suffered interference from the pirate stations. Only Radio Caroline continued to broadcast, and moved its offices from London to Amsterdam and Paris. For 21-year-old Alan Thompson, an electronic-industry trainee, the end of stations like Caroline and Radio London was a major issue. "A lot of young people were very disenchanted with Labour for killing off pirate radio."

A month after closing the "pirates", the BBC opened up their new radio formats with the old Light Programme splitting into the new Radio 1 and Radio 2, while the Third Programme became Radio 3 and Radio 4 took over from the Home Service. At 7am on Saturday, September 30, DJ Tony Blackburn launched Radio 1 with the Move's 'Flowers In The Rain', which went down in history as the first disc to be played on the new station.

In another corner of Europe, Gibraltar took to the polls to decide whether to remain as part of Great Britain or join Spain, and a 95% turnout resulted in more than 99% of the rock's inhabitants deciding to remain British.

October began with the death of folk legend Woody Guthrie, the man who inspired Bob Dylan while, in Bolivia, Marxist revolutionary Che Guevara was shot and killed. His body lay undiscovered for over 30 years before being exhumed and buried in Cuba.

The Beatles were offered – and turned down – £1 million to return to the stage for live shows at New York's Shea Stadium, while the first so-called rock musical, *Hair*, opened off-Broadway in New York, complete with nudity, swearing and an integrated cast.

A new Abortion Bill was introduced in Britain, which allowed licensed practitioners to perform legal operations, which were also free on the NHS. For motorists there was the introduction of the breathalyser to reduce cases of drink-driving, while all new cars had to be fitted with seat belts, although there was no law making drivers wear them.

October saw more anti-war protests in America with over 100,000 people joining a march that ended in a rally at the Lincoln Memorial in Washington DC, while November began with America voting in its first African-America mayor of a major city when Carl B Stokes took up office in Cleveland Ohio. Over in the Soviet Union, the country was celebrating the 50th anniversary of the October Soviet Revolution in 1917, which ended the rule of the Romanov dynasty and saw Vladimir Lenin seize power.

As the BBC opened its first local radio station in Leicester, so *Rolling Stone* magazine was launched in America, with John Lennon on the cover in a pose from the film *How I Won the War*. The magazine's title was taken from a Muddy Waters song, and the first edition came with a freebie roach clip.

In November The Beatles changed the name of their business from Beatles Limited to Apple Music Limited, and early in the following month opened the Apple Boutique in London's Baker Street, which had been designed and kitted out at a cost of £100,000 by the Anglo-Dutch team known as The Fool.

On December 4 South African surgeon Dr Christian Barnard performed the world's first heart-transplant operation in Cape Town, when he removed the heart from road-traffic victim Denise Darvall and gave it to shopkeeper Louis Washansky, who survived for 18 days.

In the run-up to Christmas 1967, soul singer Otis Redding and four members of his group, The Bar-Kays, died when their plane crashed into Lake Monona in Wisconsin on December 10.

The release of the film *Guess Who's Coming To Dinner*, which focused on the engagement of a black man to a white girl, came just six months after a law forbidding interracial marriage in 17 American states was finally lifted.

In Britain, 1967 closed with the final edition of one of television's longest-running pop-music shows, as *Juke Box Jury*, which began in 1959, ended with regular host David Jacobs in the chair. At its peak the programme drew audiences of over 12 million and, in 1963, when The Beatles appeared, the figure jumped to a massive 23 million.

Left: DJ Tony Blackburn adjusts his headphones ahead of the launch of the BBC's new premier music station, Radio 1.

Following pages: Crowds gathered outside the Apple boutique in London for the great clothes giveaway in July 1968.

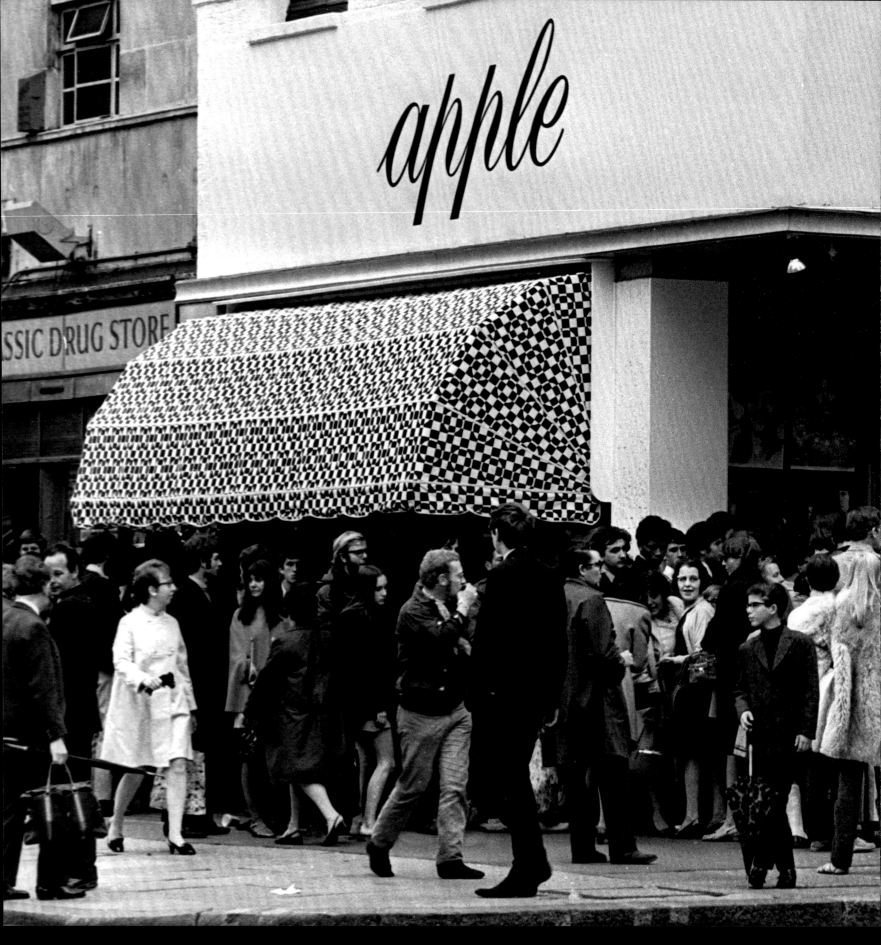

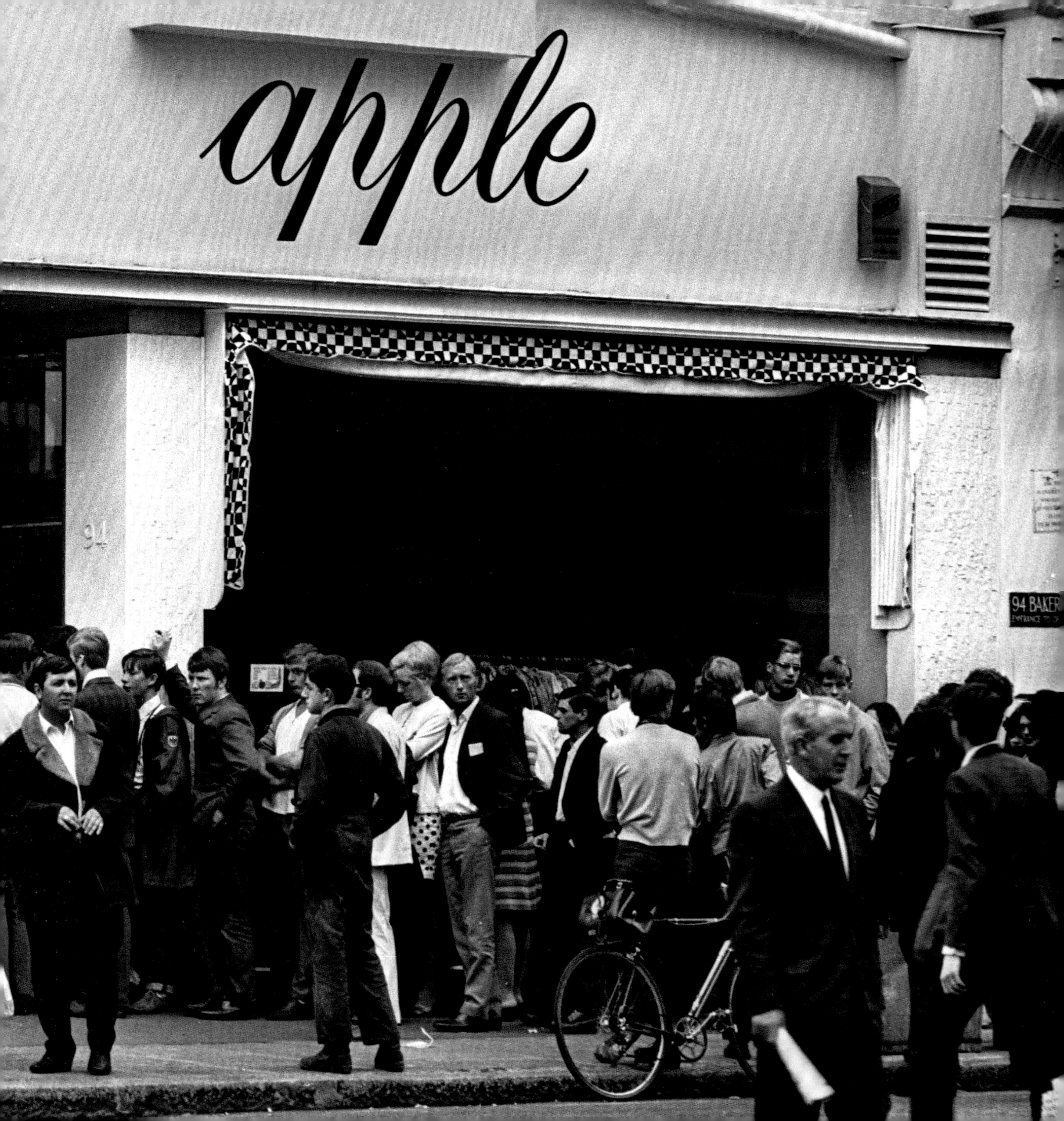
apple
94
94 BAKER

THERE'S A RIOT GOIN' ON

After the year of flower power, love and peace, people turned their attention to the bigger issues of the day and began to gather together and raise their voices in protest against war, inequality and even governments – and not always peacefully.

For barrister-turned-author and feminist Liz Woodcraft, who was studying at Birmingham University back then, 1968 was "a year when we thought and hoped the world would change." The change that she hoped for was set against a backdrop of unrest around the world as students and disenchanted citizens made themselves heard in the hope that authority in all its forms listened and, more importantly, took notice.

When she turned 18 in 1968, Woodcraft, who grew up in Chelmsford as the daughter of a senior trade-union official and Essex County Councillor, saw that things had started to happen. "It was a beginning of change, but not exactly as we had hoped and it wouldn't be until the seventies when things really took off."

At the same time, Ray Connolly, a music journalist on the *London Evening Standard* in 1968, was also keeping an eye on world affairs. "I was aware of what was going on. 1967 had been the year of peace and all that bollocks, and it was followed by the so-called year of revolution which was even more nonsense. It was radical chic revolution."

Nevertheless, there were people throughout Britain, all around Europe and across the United States who were determined to stand up for what they believed was right.

Opposite: Protestors and police clash during the Poor People's Campaign in Washington, DC, against the backdrop of the Supreme Court.

Left: Police and protesters clashed in Derry in Northern Ireland in October 1968.

The first hint of change came as early as January 5, 1968, when Alexander Dubček was elected first secretary of the Communist Party in Czechoslovakia, a country which was a member of the Warsaw Pact, a military alliance set up by Eastern European countries in 1955. Despite potential problems with his Communist neighbours and allies, he was keen to introduce a series of radical reforms and new freedoms in the country.

At the same time in neighbouring Poland, 300 students from the University of Warsaw took the streets to protest against censorship and their country's economic problems. Their concerns brought a violent reaction from the state authorities but, undaunted, the protesters rallied again in March and this time demonstrations were held in Krakow, Gdansk and other cities.

After 20 days of organized protesting across the country, the Polish government decided that the way to end it all was by closing every university and arresting over 1,000 students. In nearby Netherlands, there was a peaceful protest against the Vietnam War during February but it was an almost isolated incident in a country that, according to Roel Kruize, who worked for the EMI -owned Bovema company, was feeling comfortable. "The country's economy was booming and a lot of people could suddenly afford a TV and a car. We also had a stable and quite balanced political system where the majority of people felt themselves represented."

However, during the year, the Netherlands did experience a number of non-violent demonstrations when the provocative Provo movement created their "white bicycle" plan to improve Amsterdam's transport system but, says Kruize, "Things never really got out of hand;

"The protest against the Vietnam War became a global event as it was such an appalling war"

Gered Mankowitz

there were demonstrations by students wanting involvement in their education and strikes by the building industry, but no real riots, no real uproar."

Meanwhile, in Orangeburg, South Carolina, the US civil-rights movement staged a peaceful protest in February at the whites-only All-Star bowling alley, which moved on to the campus of South Carolina State College where around 200 students held a demonstration. Officers from the state highway patrol were called and three students were shot and killed by the police.

Two months later – on April 4 – civil-rights leader Martin Luther King was assassinated on the balcony of his Memphis hotel room by James Earl Ray. It led to riots throughout America's major cities as people mourned King's death and rallied to the cause of the growing civil-rights movement, which now focused attention on the more radical Black Power and Black Panther organizations.

Within days of King's murder, riots erupted in Washington DC against poor living conditions for black people, segregation, inequality and poor education. Known as the "Holy Week of Uprising", the protests spread across the US, with looting and buildings being set on fire in Chicago and Baltimore. President Lyndon Johnson responded by sending over 13,000 federal troops to quell the disturbances, which left 39 people dead, over 1,000 injured and more than 6,000 arrested.

When King's funeral took place in Atlanta, Georgia on April 9, 150,000 formed a three-and-a-half-mile funeral procession through the city. Two months later, Ray was arrested at London's Heathrow Airport and sentenced to 99 years in prison, despite claims that he was set-up as part of a conspiracy by white supremacists.

In the immediate aftermath of King's killing, members of the Black Panthers organized an ambush of police in Oakland, California, which resulted in two officers being seriously wounded and the Panthers' 18-year-old Treasurer Bobby Hutton being killed.

For London-based photographer Gered Mankowitz, the death of King reminded him of events he had witnessed first-hand years earlier. "I was aware of the racial tension in America because when I went there in 1965 with the Rolling Stones I did see the segregation that existed back then."

Mankowitz also discussed the situation with one of rock's superstars when he was photographing him in London in 1967. "I talked to Jimi Hendrix about it a bit and also shared studio space with a couple of people who were quite politically active, and through them I became aware of some of the movements and events."

The demonstrations that brought killings to the streets of America were a long way removed from the biggest mass protest to hit London for decades, when over 10,000 people descended on Grosvenor Square – the home of the US Embassy – on March 17. They were there to protest against the Vietnam War, which America had been actively fighting since 1964, and by 1968 had dispatched over 500,000 troops to fight against the communist forces of North Vietnam.

While thousands gathered in central London to voice their disapproval, Liz Woodcraft was not among them. "I was still living at home and my mum just would not let me go because she was concerned about my safety." However, a number of Woodcraft's fellow students from Colchester Technical College did go and, as Woodcraft recalls, "One of them was arrested even though I don't think she really believed in the cause."

Mankowitz was another who never made it to Grosvenor Square but recalls his feelings about the conflict. "The protest against the Vietnam War became a global event as it was such an appalling war, such a ghastly thing that it enveloped so many people in different countries.

"The feedback from my friends who went was mixed – a lot of bravado and a genuine sense of it being important to protest. There was also a sense of impending danger from what was seen as an over-reaction by the police." And it seems that the rock photographer's pals who were there were prepared for violence. "I think there were a lot of protestors who were pleased that it blew up in the way it did, and one mate had taken lessons from a very dodgy Irish friend about how to disable a horse by punching it on the nose."

Pop star Peter Asher, half of the hit-making duo Peter and Gordon, did make it to Grosvenor Square, as he explains. "We noticed all that was going as it was in the newspapers and I got involved in those 1968 riots." Meanwhile students at North Essex Poly in East London were also making a statement as student Alan

---

Left: Tanks drove into Wenceslas Square in the summer of 1968 to end the so-called 'Prague Spring' revolution.

109

Thompson recalls, "They painted graffiti against the war in Vietnam all over the walls, but they weren't very active apart from that."

Writing in the *Daily Mail* in 2008, Peter Hitchens recalled his day at the demo, aged just 17. "I vividly remember the intense, rapid, thrilling moments as the demonstration against the Vietnam War turned nasty; the sudden, urgent shoving, the unsettling feeling of being surrounded by strangers, supposedly my allies, the clatter of hooves, the struggle to save myself from being pushed to the ground."

At the end of the day, 200 people were arrested and, while there were no fatalities, over 90 people were injured. Earlier in the year, American politician and women's-rights advocate Jeanette Rankin had led her "brigade" of 5,000 women on a an anti-Vietnam War march in Washington, while in April in Boston, 1,000 men burned their draft cards – which required them to report for duty in the US Armed Forces – in front of 15,000 supporters.

However, despite the news coverage and demonstrations, the Vietnam War still failed to make an impact with much of Britain's youth. Steve Harley – later to lead Cockney Rebel to chart success – was starting out as a 17-year-old old trainee journalist. "Despite being a young newshound the world stage was an altogether bigger stage and I was focused on what was happening in my local area. Vietnam was seen as America's problem, I didn't know a lot about it, and I was never moved to protest – it wasn't my way."

Mick Brown, later to write for *Rolling Stone* magazine and the *Daily Telegraph*, recalls that, while news about American events was limited, there was another important medium for a teenager living in the suburbs of London. "Rock music became the lingua franca for young people around the world, and musicians did carry the protest message."

While the war in Vietnam raged on, and more and more American citizens became disenchanted with their country's efforts to stem the Communist movement in South East Asia, so President Lyndon B Johnson's popularity

declined. For Woodcraft, a self-confessed radical member of the Labour Party, America's policy stood for one thing. "It was a continuation of powerful Americans trying to rule the world with capitalism, and I made it my business [to protest]."

And she and her fellow protesters made their feelings clear with the cry, "Hey, hey, LBJ, how many kids did you kill today?" On May 10, Johnson agreed to an opening round of peace talks in Paris to try to bring to an end the long-running war.

Jonathan Morrish was in his last year at college in Bristol in 1968, and explains that Vietnam was never on the school curriculum. "We were definitely cocooned in an English public school where it never became part of our lessons. In Britain we did not have a sense of what Vietnam really meant to a generation in America – they really did have something to rail against while we had nobody in the war."

At the same time, people in Rome joined in with their own anti-Vietnam War protests while the Spanish gathered in Madrid to demonstrate against the military regime of their fascist leader General Francisco Franco, who had come to power in 1939.

The protest movement was also taking hold in Germany where there was dissatisfaction with the authoritarianism of the West German government, student poverty and proposed laws to restrict civil rights and freedom of movement in the event of an emergency. Under the banner of the SDS (Socialist Germen Students) – with Rudi Dutschke leading the movement – a growing band of demonstrators took to the streets.

An attempt to assassinate Dutschke brought increased unrest, and resulted in two protestors being killed and 400 injured, and saw 80,000 students, union workers and citizens gather in Berlin in May 1968. Even so, the protests soon declined and the government's emergency laws were eventually passed.

The world's attention was also drawn to Paris in the May when 800,000 people marched on the French capital and 10 million workers

went on a national strike. The focus of their attention were the policies of the government led by President Charles De Gaulle, coupled with concerns about capitalism, consumerism and American imperialism.

Earlier poets, musicians and students had occupied Paris University and, when that was closed by the authorities, students and teachers from the Sorbonne University joined the protests, while the country's far left and communist groups sought to bring down the government. Surprisingly, even though he had secretly fled Paris at the height of the troubles, De Gaulle was re-elected in June with an increased majority.

A year earlier, Woodcraft had worked as an au pair in France and developed "a love affair" with the country, which meant she took a particular interest in the events of May 1968. "I worked in London during that summer and met a guy in a second-hand book shop who was French and we got talking. He had been on some of the demos with a friend who had been blinded by tear gas during the riots."

Two months after the murder of Martin Luther King, America suffered another political killing when Robert F Kennedy, the Senator for New York and former US Attorney General, was shot in Los Angeles on June 5. Kennedy, brother of US President John F Kennedy, who had been assassinated in 1963, had just won California's support to be the Democratic Presidential nomination in the November elections. He was killed by Palestinian Sirhan Sirhan who was arrested five days layer in Los Angeles and sentenced to life imprisonment.

American author and academic Kenneth Womack confirms that Sirhan was opposed to Senator Kennedy's support for Israel and this his action "led to a power vacuum that effectively destabilized the anti-war faction of the Democratic Party"

Before he was assassinated, Martin Luther King had been actively involved in organizing a Poor People's March on Washington DC, in an effort to gain justice and support for the poor people of America. It was planned to run

from May 14 through to June 24 but, following King's murder, it was postponed until June 19 when 50,000 people congregated in America's capital city.

Six months after he had initiated his reforms, Czech leader Alexander Dubček reiterated his determination for the progressive policies he saw as part of a "socialist democratic revolution" but, a month later, in August, the leaders of the U.S.S.R. decided enough was enough.

The men from the Kremlin, concerned about their position at the head of the Eastern bloc countries, sent 750,000 Warsaw Pact troops, 6,500 tanks and 800 planes into Czechoslovakia to deal with any resistance in what was considered to be the biggest operation in Europe since World War II.

There were isolated pockets of resistance and silent vigils, including one in Prague's famous Wenceslas Square on August 28, but

Czechoslovakia's so-called "Prague Spring" was over and so was Dubček's career. He was replaced as head of the Czech Communist Party in early 1969, sent to Turkey to be his country's ambassador and finally expelled from the Communist Party in 1970, but his legacy was the eventual creation of the Czech and Slovak republics in 1992.

If the Vietnam War did not have a profound effect on Steve Harley, the events in Czechoslovakia in 1968 did, as the man who hit No. 1 in the UK charts with 'Make Me Smile (Come Up and See Me)' in 1975 recalls. "I soaked up this story. The Russian invasion of Prague was part of my life as it was almost on our doorstep compared to the United States. We had the Iron Curtain and we were all scared to death of the Russians – there was a great fear of the Russian bear."

In August 1968, two months after the death of Robert Kennedy, the US Democratic Party

held its National Convention in Chicago, where Herbert Humphrey was elected to be the party's Presidential candidate alongside Edmund Muskie. According to Womack, "The summer's awful events reached their nadir in Chicago where thousands of people gathered to protest [against] the Vietnam War and the policies of [Democratic] President Lyndon B Johnson."

The 10,000 protestors included Students for a Democratic Society and the Youth International Party (the "yippies"), and their violent confrontations saw Chicago Mayor Richard J Daley order over 12,000 police officers to respond with clubs, dogs and tear gas. The rioting went on for three days and was seen by millions on American television

Above: The National Guard is sent in to patrol the streets of Orangeburg, South Carolina following the deaths of three black students.

and, according to Womack, "The convention's tragic turn of events weakened support for Herbert Humphrey."

The autumn of 1968 saw Woodcraft arrive at university in Birmingham, England's second city, where it became clear to her, and her fellow students, that things had to change. "Those were the days when you sat in rows in great halls and people lectured at you and some of them were very bad teachers. As a reaction to that we held a sit-in, which was all about student representation and teaching. Students were beginning to feel their power – it was happening all over the country – and as a result we did succeed in getting student representation within the university."

Students were also protesting in Mexico where, on October 2 – just ten days before the 1968 Olympics opened – over 10,000 men, women and children gathered in a suburb of Mexico City to protest against the government of the ruling Institutional Revolutionary Party (PRI). The crowd were confronted by armed police and military, who opened fire, killing dozens and wounding hundreds more.

During the Olympic Games that followed, American athletes Tommie Smith and John Carlos – winners of the gold and bronze medals in the 200 metres – stood on the victory podium and raised black-gloved fists during the playing of their national anthem. Their action was seen as support of the Black Power movement, and both were expelled from the Olympic Games. Explaining his actions, Smith said, "We are black and proud of being black. Black America will understand what we did tonight."

In London on Sunday, October 27, a second anti-Vietnam War protest took place, seven months after 10,000 people had gathered in Grosvenor Square. This time more than 30,000 marchers made for London's Hyde Park for a peaceful rally, while a break-away group of around 6,000 descended on the US Embassy where they were met by a wall of police

Reporting on the days' events in 1968, the *Guardian* newspaper said, "At the height of the melee the police line nearly gave way, but it was immediately reinforced, and no demonstrators came nearer than 50 yards to the Embassy building. During scuffles in which a police line in South Audley Street was broken through some of the demonstrators turned their banner stakes into spears, which they hurled at the police. Fireworks were constantly thrown, both into the crowds and into the police lines."

The newspaper concluded, "Last night, as the marchers retreated in front of the advancing police line, Grosvenor Square was a litter of lost shoes, broken glass, torn banners, and discarded clothing."

While she wasn't in Hyde Park or Grovesnor Square, Woodcraft was in London that weekend as part of a student sit-in at the London School of Economics and Political Science. "I assume there must have been some sort of a cry that went out for people to go and support their sit-in so I hitched down the London."

In fact, the students at the LSE decided to sit-in as a protest against a decision taken by the School's director to close the building, fearing crowds of anti-Vietnam War demonstrators would invade the site. The sit-in began on Thursday, October 24 – three days before the planned Hyde Park rally – when 3,000 students from around the country took over the LSE in London's Holborn, and stayed there until Sunday night – during which time they secured it against intruders and cleaned the building.

College boy Jonathan Morrish – later to become head of PR at CBS Records and Sony Music – looks back on the politics and protests that shaped 1968 and the part played by two major rock albums released close to year's end. "I think the White Album and the Stones' *Beggars Banquet* both reflect the innocence that had been lost with the assassination of political figures in America, and what was going on in Europe."

Opposite and above: Revolution was a worldwide phenomenon, with demonstrations erupting in (clockwise from top left) San Francisco, London and Frankfurt, to name just a few.

1968: REVOLUTION'S IN THE AIR

In a year of growing political turmoil and general unrest, music and musicians took a major step towards the revolution, as artists joined with their fans in the search for change – and a better world.

JANUARY

The US music magazine *Billboard* reported on the first day of the New Year that Americans had spent more than $1 billion on records during 1967, with albums (192 million) outselling singles (187 million) for the first time. Around the same time, the British music-trade paper *Record Retailer* carried a story in its January 3 edition, announcing that The Beatles would launch their own record label – Apple Records – during the summer.

For Anglo-Irish poet Cecil Day-Lewis (the father of Oscar-winning actor Sir Daniel Day-Lewis), the New Year began with him being named as Britain's 16th Poet Laureate in succession to John Masefield. BBC TV's long-running gardening programme *Gardeners' World* first aired on January 5 with Ken Burras hosting a show from Oxford Botanical Gardens, a year before its best-known host, Percy Thrower, took over. And January saw the new Ford Escort car being introduced as the replacement for the Ford Anglia. Launched at the Brussels Motor Show as a pan-European car, the standard saloon version cost £666.

Britain's Prime Minister, Harold Wilson, chose the first week of January to get behind a growing "I'm Backing Britain" campaign,

which urged workers to spend an extra 30 minutes at work for no pay, in an effort to boost the country's competitiveness. Despite trade-union officials being suspicious of the cause, people carried shopping bags and badges and T-shirts with the message "I'm Backing Britain", and entertainer Bruce Forsyth released an 'I'm Backing Britain' single, which sold for just 5 shillings (25p) instead of the usual 7s .4d (37p). It only sold 7,300 copies and, within months, the whole initiative had fizzled out.

A year after winning the first-ever Super Bowl, the Green Bay Packers took the prize again when they defeated the Oakland Rangers 33-14 in front of 75,000 fans in Miami on January 14. A week later, America's NBC TV network launched a new fast-action comedy show entitled *Rowan & Martin's Laugh-In*. Starring Dan Rowan and Dick Martin, the first show featured Goldie Hawn and Judy Carne and the series ran until 1973 – a total of 140 episodes.

Two submarines – one from Israel and one from France – sank mysteriously in the Mediterranean Sea in the final week of January. The Israeli sub Dakar, bought from the British in 1975, was lost with its crew of 69 while France's Minerve went down with 52 on board.

BORN
West Indian cricketer Jimmy Adams (9)
model and activist Heather Mills (12)
British rapper Tricky (27)
King Felipe VI of Spain (30)

DIED
Japanese Olympic marathon runner
Kokichi Tsuburaya (9)
Canadian ice hockey star Bill Masterson (15)
English actress Virginia Maskell (25)

The US Air Force also suffered a disaster when a B-52 bomber crashed into ice off Greenland while carrying four hydrogen bombs, which, according Defence Department officials, were "unarmed" and there was "no danger of a nuclear explosion."

With founding member Syd Barret becoming "crazier and crazier", according to Roger Waters, Pink Floyd opted not to collect their guitarist and songwriter for a gig in Southampton on January 26. Fellow Cambridge musician David Gilmour, formerly with The Ramblers, was recruited to join what would be a five-piece group until Barrett finally left in March.

After Jimi Hendrix had been arrested and jailed overnight in Stockholm for wrecking a hotel room in early January, the month closed with The Who and The Small Faces being thrown off a plane in Australia for making an air hostess cry, while Doors' leader Jim Morrison was arrested in the car park of an adult cinema in Las Vegas and charged with vagrancy and public drunkenness.

As the month came to end, the Viet Cong army of North Vietnam launched surprise attacks across 13 cities in South Vietnam as part of what would become known as the Tet Offensive. Traditionally Tet, a celebration in Vietnam of the lunar new year, had been marked by an informal truce in the long-running Vietnam war, but the Viet Cong continued their offensive with an unsuccessful attack on the US Embassy in Saigon.

Below: Goldie Hawn (left) and Pamela Rodgers appear in the famous 'joke wall' on *Rowan & Martin's Laugh-In.*

116

BOB DYLAN RETURNS

Eighteen months after suffering serious (and mysterious) injuries in a motor-cycle accident, Bob Dylan returned to the stage at New York's Carnegie Hall on January 20, 1968.

Having reportedly broken his neck when he crashed his Triumph Bonneville 650 near his home in Woodstock, New York, on July 25, 1966, Dylan became something of a recluse as he recuperated from his injuries and apparently took stock of his career. "I was pretty wound up before the accident," was Dylan's assessment of his situation. "I probably would have died if I kept on going the way I had."

So, after spending the previous two months in the studio working on an album, he chose a sell-out memorial concert for his great hero Woody Guthrie for his return and joined Pete Seeger, Arlo Guthrie, Odetta, Richie Havens, Judy Collins and Ramblin' Jack Elliott to pay tribute to Guthrie, who had died in September 1967, aged 55.

Also playing the concert were the Hawks (billed as The Crackers, and later to be known as The Band), who had toured with Dylan in 1965 and 1966, and they accompanied Dylan as he performed a selection of Guthrie's compositions. According to *Rolling Stone* magazine's report, Dylan's appearance "broke all previous bounds even before he began to sing" and then his performance took on "a strong rock beat that had some girls in the audience boogalooing in their seats."

In the final months of 1967, Dylan released his first album since 1966 and *John Wesley Harding* was apparently completed in just three days of recording – during October and November – in Nashville, Tennessee. It immediately shot to No. 2 in America but went one better in the UK, where it topped the charts for ten consecutive weeks – and held the No. 1 spot for another three weeks in May. Steve Harley was just beginning his career as a journalist when the album came out, and he remembers his reaction to Dylan's eighth studio album. "I loved *John Wesley Harding* to death. I was in a bed-sit in Braintree in Essex where I was on the local paper and I played it on my Dansette record player. It was a beautiful album, I adored it and I wore a stylus out just continuously playing 'All Along The Watchtower'."

While Dylan issued no singles from his comeback album, Jimi Hendrix, who performed Dylan's 'Like a Rolling Stone' at the 1967 Monterey Pop Festival, chose to cover 'All Along the Watchtower', turning it into a top-twenty entry in America and a top-five hit in the UK.

JANUARY NUMBER ONES

SINGLES

'Hello Goodbye' – The Beatles (UK)

'The Ballad of Bonnie and Clyde' – Georgie Fame UK)

'Everlasting Love' – Love Affair (UK)

'Hello Goodbye' – The Beatles (US)

'Judy in Disguise (With Glasses)' – John Fred and His Playboy Band (US)

ALBUMS

Sgt Pepper's Lonely Hearts Club – The Beatles (UK)

Val Doonican Rocks but Gently – Val Doonican (UK)

The Sound of Music – Soundtrack (UK)

Pisces, Aquarius, Capricorn & Jones Ltd. – The Monkees (US)

Magical Mystery Tour – The Beatles (US)

Opposite, above: US troops take cover during the Viet Cong's January 1968 TET offensive in Vietnam.

Opposite, below: Protesters and burning cars on the streets of Prague, the capital of Czechoslovakia.

B

New from Mattel. Action sets for the fastest miniature metal cars you've ever seen!

New Hot Wheels out-race, out-stunt, out-distance any other kind of miniature car.

Stunt Action Set. Comes with California styled Hot Wheels car, dare devil loop that sends other miniature cars tumbling, ramps for jumps other cars can't make, trestle, 16 feet of special track, collector button.

Three other great sets to choose from!

Strip Action Set. Complete with Hot Wheels car, 10 feet of track, collector button.

Drag Race Action Set. Comes with 2 cars, starting and finishing gates, elimination lane merger, 30 feet of track, collector button.

Hot Curves Race Action Set. Comes with 2 Hot Wheels cars, 4 banked curves, 6 trestles, starting and finishing gates, 32 ft. of track, collector button.

Collect Hot Wheels separately, too. 16 custom styled cars to choose from!

©1968 Mattel, Inc.

Far left: MacDonald's famous 'Golden Arches' symbol was introduced in 1968 by owner Ray Kroc.

Left: The new collectible *Hot Wheels* toys were introduced by Mattel in May 1968

Below: Velvet Underground - (l to r) Lou Reed, Sterling Morrison, John Cale and Maureen Tucker – released their album *White Light White Heat* in 1968.

FEBRUARY

America's involvement in the Vietnam War suffered a setback at the very start of the month when a Viet Cong officer was executed in public following the deaths of a South Vietnamese family. Thirty-six-year-old Nguyễn Văn Lém shot and killed South Vietnamese police officer Lt Col Nguyễn Tuan, his wife, six children and his mother during the Tet Offensive and was then shot by General Nguyễn Ngoc Luan. The killing in a Saigon street was captured by US cameraman Eddie Adams and, when his photograph was published around the world, public support in the US was swayed against America's continuing involvement in the Vietnam War.

At the same time, America also saw its largest corporate merger to date when the Pennsylvania Railroad and New York Central Railroad joined forces on February 1 to create a company called Penn Central. However, within two years, the company went bankrupt in what, at the time, was the country's largest private bankruptcy.

In their February 10 issue, *MM* lauded the efforts of Los Angeles band Love and their second album, *Forever Changes*. Reviewing the UK top-thirty album – it peaked at 152 in America – the music paper describes the record as "a superb example of modern American pop music at its tasteful and purposeful."

On the very next day, a brand-new purpose-built auditorium opened in New York City. The new Madison Square Garden arena was built over Penn Station between Manhattans' 31st and 33rd Street, with a maximum capacity of over 20,000 for concerts and boxing matches.

It replaced the previous "Garden", which was built in 1925 on 8th Avenue at a cost of $4.7 million.

On February 28, at the age of just 25, American former teenage pop sensation Frankie Lymon was found dead in his grandmother's New York house. On leave from the army, Lymon died from a heroin overdose 12 years after the release – with his group the Teenagers – of their debut single 'Why Do Fools Fall In Love', which topped the British charts and sold over seven million copies worldwide.

Left: The 1968 Winter Olympics were held in Grenoble in France in February.

Below: The new 20,000 seater Madison Square Garden opened in New York.

FEBRUARY NUMBER ONES

SINGLES

'Everlasting Love' – Love Affair (UK)
'Mighty Quinn' – Manfred Mann (UK)
'Cinderella Rockafella' –
Esther & Abi Ofarim (UK)
'Green Tambourine' – The Lemon Pipers (US)
'Love Is Blue' – Paul Mauriat (US)

ALBUMS

Sgt Pepper's Lonely Hearts Club Band –
The Beatles (UK)
Greatest Hits – Four Tops (UK)
Greatest Hits – Diana Ross &
The Supremes (UK)
Magical Mystery Tour – The Beatles (US)

B

BORN
Spanish tennis star Javier Sanchez (1)
Spin Doctors' Chris Barron (5)
US actress Molly Ringwald (18)

DIED
Beat Generation author/poet Neal Cassady (4)
Blues harmonica player Little Walter Jacobs (15)
British actor/manager Sir Donald Wolfit (17)

Left: The original line-up of Fleetwood Mac pose for a playful portrait on the streets of London.

Below: US state police on guard in South Carolina following student demonstrations in February 1968.

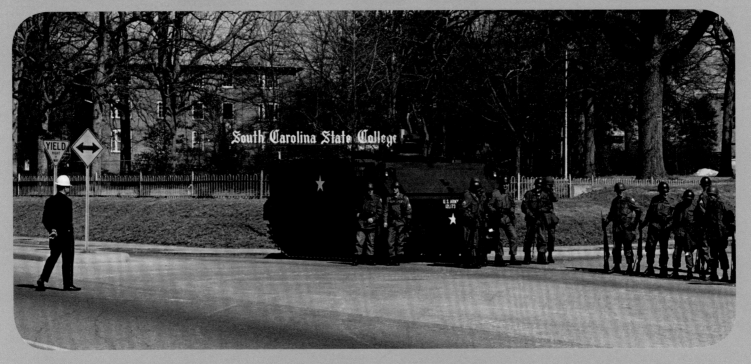

BEATLES TAKE OFF FOR INDIA

On February 16 the *Sun* newspaper carried a photograph of George Harrison, Patti Boyd, and John and Cynthia Lennon at Heathrow Airport on their way to India. The headline on the story read "Beatles Fly Off To Do Hard Thinking" and carried a quote from Harrison saying, "There is no question of a bed of nails – that is for yogi man – but it is not easy living."

Four days later, the *Daily Mail* reported that Paul McCartney, Jane Asher plus Ringo and Maureen Starr were also on their way to India and, under the heading "Off For A Spot of Meditation", suggested that The Beatles would meet up "at the Yogi's cold bath and meditation course on the banks of the Ganges."

In fact, all four Beatles were off to the Maharishi Mahesh Yogi's Himalayan retreat, located 150 miles from Delhi at Rishikesh. There, together with the Beach Boys Mike Love, folk singer Donovan, American actress Mia Farrow and her sister Prudence, they spent their time, according to McCartney, "just eating, sleeping and meditating – with the occasional little lecture from the Maharishi thrown in."

The group had first met the Maharishi in London in the summer of 1967, and then joined him for a course at Bangor University before agreeing to travel out to India for a planned three-month visit, which ended up lasting a little over six weeks.

The Beatles spent time much of their writing the songs that would make up the bulk of their next album release, with Lennon explaining, "I wrote some of my best songs while I was there. It was a nice scene. The experience was worth it, if only for the songs that came out but it could have been the desert or Ben Nevis."

Harrison, who was the most committed to the philosophies of the East and the Maharishi's Academy of Transcendental Meditation, commented, "I believe I have already extended my life by twenty years. I believe there are bods up here in the Himalayas who have lived for centuries."

Living in stone cottages with twin beds, The Beatles and the other guests enjoyed cold-water baths and followed a vegetarian diet before Starr opted out after just ten days. McCartney lasted five weeks, while Lennon and Harrison were the last to leave after a story spread around the village that the Maharishi had made a pass at one of the female visitors.

"Someone started a nasty rumour about Maharishi, a rumour that swept the media for years," recalls Harrison. "The story stirred up a situation. John had wanted to leave anyway so that forced him into a position of thinking 'now we've got a good reason to get out of here.'"

While the Beatles were away in India, journalist Don Short, who had covered The Beatles' adventures for the *Daily Mirror* for some years and had travelled to Rishikesh, wrote a feature for the *MM* and asked the question, "Have they gone off their heads?" Short's answer was "no" and he further explained, "The trend-setting Liverpool foursome believe, and very firmly believe, that a trend towards transcendental meditation could mean the solution to all of today's world problems."

The journalist also gave his opinion of the Maharishi, saying, "I liked him instantly and he has a knack of creating a human bond which cannot be broken or harmed by what others may think." However, following the spread of rumours and their own early departure, The Beatles were asked to clarify their position regarding the Indian mystic and, speaking in New York in May 1968, McCartney explained, "We made a mistake. We thought there was more to him than there was. He's human. We thought at first he wasn't."

MARCH

Five years before it would appear in London's West End, the Tim Rice and Andrew Lloyd Webber musical *Joseph and His Amazing Technicolor Dreamcoat* had its debut performance at Coley Preparatory School in Hammersmith, West London on March 1. It was a 20-minute "pop cantata", which was then played at the Westminster Central Hall in May and, eventually – as a 30-minute piece – at St Paul's Cathedral in November.

Britain's long-established coal-mining industry suffered a major setback on March 2, when the Baggeridge Colliery near Sedgley in the West Midlands closed. During its 300-year history, the colliery had been an important part of Britain's Industrial Revolution, which began in the 1760s.

French artist Marcel Duchamp and American musician John Cage met up in Toronto on March 5 to play a revolutionary "musical chess" match involving the use of photoresistors on the board. The avant-garde musician Cage, aged 56, lost to the 80-year-old conceptual artist and chess fanatic. A day later, American fans of the CBS show *Lost in Space* tuned in to see the series come to an end after 83 shows.

The first official biography of The Beatles was published in early March, and author Hunter Davies told the *Sun* newspaper that the hardest part of his dealings with the "fab four" "was gaining their confidence and friendship." He also confided that he had to prepare himself

for their moods, explaining that John Lennon would have days of not talking, while George Harrison would prefer to practice the sitar, and Ringo Starr wanted to play billiards. Finally, he said that Paul McCartney would take his dog – "and me" – on long, silent walks.

After 158 years as a British colony, the island nation of Mauritus achieved independence on March 12, but retained Queen Elizabeth II as its head of state. Three days later, Britain's Labour Government, led by Harold Wilson,

First man in space Soviet cosmonaut Yuri Gagarin (above) was honoured with a state funeral in Moscow's Red Square (right) following his death in a plane crash.

LADY MADONNA/ THE INNER LIGHT

The Beatles had been away from the recording studios for over two months when they gathered in Abbey Road for an afternoon and evening session on Saturday, February 3, to record a new single as a follow up to 'Hello Goodbye'.

The entire 12 hours in Studio Three were spent on a new Fats Domino-inspired rocker called 'Lady Madonna', which featured Paul McCartney's double-track piano. A second session three days later involved four saxophone players – legendary London jazz-club owner Ronnie Scott plus Bill Jackman, Bill Povey and Harry Klein – playing notes and chords they wrote down as McCartney ran through the song on the piano.

Explaining the song, McCartney once said that Lady Madonna started out as the Virgin Mary, and then became a working-class woman and added, "It's really a tribute to the mother figure, it's a tribute to women."

Released on March 15, 'Lady Madonna' swept to No. 1 in the UK but stalled at No. 4 in America, despite selling over a million copies in the week of release and *Billboard* magazine declaring it was "a powerful blues rocker."

In the *Daily Mail*, Virginia Ironside also announced that the new single was "pure rock", while *London Evening Standard* pop critic Ray Connolly wrote, "...if there's going to be a rock 'n' roll revival we should have realized that The Beatles would turn out the best damn rock record made in years."

However, Britain's two leading music papers took different views, with *NME* man Derek Johnson writing, "It isn't the raw blatant rock of the group's early days, it's controlled, polished and impeccably produced. In other words it's updated sophisticated rock." On the other hand, *MM*'s Chris Welch suggested that the record was "Not so much a rock 'n' roll song more an impressionist view of the riotous music of all our yesterday. This time I think it's about some bird lying in bed and mending her stockings – I think."

George Harrison's raga 'The Inner Light' appeared as the B-side to 'Lady Madonna', and was his first song to appear on a Beatles single. It features lyrics inspired by a poem of the same name from the Tao Te Ching, a piece of 6th-century Chinese classic text strongly linked to Taoism. Harrison began recording the song in EMI India's studio in Bombay on January 12 – with more than a dozen local Indian musicians – and finished it off in Abbey Road in two sessions in February.

lost one of its longest-serving ministers when Foreign Secretary George Brown resigned. A disagreement over the handling of the country's financial position, following devaluation the previous year, led to a major row and the former Secretary of State and Shadow Home Secretary left the government.

America welcomed a new candidate into the Presidential race on March 16 when New York Senator and former Attorney General Robert F Kennedy threw his hat into the ring, following the decision by 36th President Lyndon B Johnson not to seek re-election.

A decision by the British Government in 1967 to introduce breath tests to curb the rate of drink-driving was vindicated in a March 21 report, that showed road deaths in the UK had fallen by 23% in the first three months since the law's introduction.

The first human to go into outer space, Yuri Gargarin, died when his MiG-15 jet crashed on March 27. The Soviet cosmonaut took his *Vostok* space craft into orbit around the earth in April 1961 and, following his death, aged 34, his ashes were sealed in a tomb in the wall of the Kremlin in Moscow's Red Square.

On a cheerier note, the Bee Gees topped the bill for the first time on a UK tour, and opened proceedings at London's Royal Festival Hall with a 67-piece orchestra and a 50-strong band from the Royal Air Force.

Right: American jazz trumpeter Miles Davis starred at the first Montreux Jazz Festival in Switzerland.

APRIL

The first week of March saw the opening of two new movies in America. *2001: A Space Odyssey* was written, directed and produced by Stanley Kubrick, and introduced the world to HAL, the on-board computer. It was followed by *Planet Of The Apes*, starring Charlton Heston, and the film, adapted from Pierre Boulle's 1963 novel, took an estimated $22 million at the box office in North America.

Nearer to home, America launched its *Apollo 6* spacecraft – via a *Saturn 5* rocket – on April 4, and the final unmanned Apollo mission orbited the earth three times during its nine-hour flight. This happened just two days before two major stars from planet Earth met up in Las Vegas.

During Welsh singer Tom Jones' appearance at the Flamingo Hotel, Elvis Presley, his wife Priscilla and eight friends took their seats for the midnight show. Reports from the hotel's lounge said that Presley led the audience in a standing ovation and later told Jones, "Man, you are the greatest!"

At the same time, rival British hitmaker Cliff Richard was beaten into second place in the Eurovision Song Contest when 'Congratulations' lost out to Spain's Massiel with 'La La La'. There was some compensation for Richard, as the song took him back to the top of the UK chart for the first time in three years.

Early in April, British singing star Petula Clark was having a more difficult time in America, after she actually touched the arm of

Left: Controversial rock musical Hair opened on Broadway at New York's Wagner Theatre in April.

Right: Million selling duo Paul Simon (l) and Art Garfunkel topped the charts in the US and UK in 1968.

singer Harry Belafonte during his appearance on her ABC TV special. The show's sponsors, the US car company Chrysler, went into melt down and demanded changes to the show following what they called 'inter-racial touching'. Their request for a different 'non-touching' take to be used was rejected by Ms Clark and her husband, Claude Wolff, who produced the TV special, and the original sequence was included in the final version of the show

The former lawyer-turned-Liberal politician, Pierre Trudeau, won the election to become Canada's Prime Minister and, during two periods in office – 1968–1979 and 1980–1984 – the man who launched 'Trudeauism' became his country's third-longest-serving leader.

Scottish racing legend and double Formula 1 world champion Jim Clark was killed at West Germany's Hockenheim circuit on April 7, when his Lotus 48 car left the track and hit a tree at 170mph. Clark had won a record number of 25 grand prix races, and in 2009 was placed first in a newspaper poll to find the greatest Formula 1 driver.

Meanwhile, in New Zealand 54 people lost their lives on April 10, when the ferry *Wahine* hit a reef in Wellington harbour and sank during cyclone Giselle, which brought winds of up to 200mph to the capital city located on the country's North Island.

The following day, US President Lyndon B Johnson signed the 1968 Civil Rights Act, which provided equal housing opportunities and rights for all people, irrespective of race, religion or nationality. It was introduced during the country's race riots, which had followed the killing of Martin Luther King.

London Bridge had been built across the River Thames back in 1831, but on April 18 it was sold to American businessman Robert P McCulloch for £1 million. He had it taken apart, shipped to the US and then re-built brick by brick – at a cost of $7 million – at Lake Havasu in Arizona, where it opened in 1971.

BORN

US actress Patricia Arquette (8)
South Korean tennis star Grace Kim (14)
British world champion boxer
Richie Woodhall (17)

DIED

Ukrainian conductor/composer
Boris Lyatoshynsky (15)
RCA music executive Steve Sholes, who
recorded Elvis Presley (22)
American actor, writer and producer
Tommy Noonan (24)

Left: Martin Luther King (2nd from r) on the balcony of his Memphis motel in April 1968.

Right: Enoch Powell's notoriously hateful "rivers of blood" speech cost the Conservative politician his job.

Following pages: Stanley Kubrick's epic science fiction film *2001: A Space Odyssey* took the world by storm after its opening in April 1968.

British Tory politician Enoch Powell caused a major outrage when he gave a speech at a Conservative Party meeting in Birmingham on April 20. Criticizing the idea of mass immigration into the UK, his talk became known as "the rivers of blood" speech and led to him being fired from the Government by Prime Minister Edward Heath.

Student Liz Woodcraft recalls that the speech was used in a philosophy lecture at Birmingham University, and explains, "It was an exercise in bad logic and we dissected the speech to show the fault with his argument." Another student, Alan Thompson, remembers that the speech came when "racial tension between the immigrant West Indians and some white English was a feature, although the huge number of mixed-race people in the London area at the time showed that they were not always at loggerheads."

For Thompson, who worked for the electronics company Plessey (whilst also studying at college), there were clear signs of segregation in the workplace. "I was knocked back by the three-tier system operated at Plessey where there were separate toilets and canteens for hourly, weekly and monthly-paid staff. There was also a definite policy about not giving jobs to black people – they could apply and be interviewed, but would never get the job."

Britain was introduced to its first decimal coins on April 23 when 15 million 10p coins and 20 million 5p coins went into circulation, alongside the existing one shilling and two shilling florin pieces – and ahead of complete decimalization in February 1971. On the same day in France, Europe's first-ever heart-transplant operation took place at Paris's Las Pitie Hospital where a three man team led by Dr Christian Cabrol gave a new heart to 66-year-old truck driver Clovis Roblain, who sadly died before the end of the month.

Meanwhile in America, the first rock musical, *Hair*, opened at the Wagner Theatre on New York's Broadway, with actors such as Meat Loaf, Keith Caradine and Ben Veeren among the cast.

B

APRIL NUMBER ONES

SINGLES

'Lady Madonna' – The Beatles (UK)

'Congratulations' – Cliff Richard (UK)

'What a Wonderful World' –
Louis Armstrong (UK)

'(Sittin' on) The Dock of the Bay' –
Otis Redding (US)

'Honey' – Bobby Goldsboro (US)

ALBUMS

John Wesley Harding – Bob Dylan (UK)

The Graduate – Soundtrack (US)

Above: Sly (3rd from left) and his Family Stone who hit the charts with 'Dance To The Music' in 1968.

Below: *Planet Of The Apes* – starring Charlton Heston and Roddy McDowell – set new box office records in 1968.

S&G'S DOUBLE TOP

Paul Simon and Art Garfunkel famously met at High School in New York in 1956, and then formed the duo Tom & Jerry – and released their debut single 'Hey Schoolgirl' a year later.

A decade on, now performing as Simon & Garfunkel, they released their fourth studio album *Bookends,* which they had started recording in 1966 and completed in 1968. Midway through their work, filmmaker Mike Nicols asked the duo to work on the soundtrack for his up-coming film *The Graduate,* and Simon came up with a new song originally entitled 'Mrs Roosevelt', which was changed to 'Mrs Robinson'.

The soundtrack album to *The Graduate* (which starred Anne Bancroft as Mrs Robinson, Dustin Hoffman and Katharine Ross), came out in January 1968 and went to the top of the US charts for nine weeks and passed the one-million sales mark, although it peaked at No. 3 in the UK. Among the tracks, alongside two versions of 'Mrs Robinson' – one an instrumental – was Simon's song 'The Sound Of Silence'.

Also featured was the hit single 'Scarborough Fair/Canticle' from the duo's earlier US top-twenty album *Parsley Sage Rosemary and Thyme,* alongside six instrumental tracks composed by jazz pianist Dave Grushin, who had been recruited by the album's producer, Teo Macero. Talking later, Grushin admitted, "The few things I wrote were little source-music pieces. So I sent the stuff and it was a joke. When I heard it, it was still a joke but it went through the roof. I couldn't believe it."

Released in April, Simon & Garfunkel's follow-up album, *Bookends,* took over the top spot on the US charts from *The Graduate,* spending seven weeks at No. 1 plus seven weeks at the top of the UK chart, where it replaced Tom Jones' *Delilah.*

The new album came with a longer version of 'Mrs Robinson', which then topped the singles chart in America and hit No. 4 in Britain, just as the duo played a series of sold-out dates at the Royal Festival Hall. During that visit, they walked out on BBC TV's *Top of the Pops* programme when a team of go-go girls danced to their hit.

While the soundtrack album *The Graduate* won the US Grammy award for Best Original Score For a Film, the song 'Mrs Robinson' took home Grammys for Record of the Year and Best Pop Vocal Performance by a Duo or Group.

Two years later, the duo swept the charts with their multi-award-winning album *Bridge Over Troubled Water* but, within months of its release, they had split up, although they would continue to reunite for occasional concerts.

MAY

Britain's first – and the worlds' tenth – heart-transplant operation – was carried out at the National Heart Hospital in Marylebone, London on May 3 when a team led by Dr Donald Ross operated on Frederick West, who died in June after 46 days.

Over in America, the Beach Boys started out on a nationwide tour and took with them the Maharishi Mahesh Yogi, who was booked to lecture on spiritual regeneration. After the opening night in Washington DC, the tour moved to New York, where just 300 people turned up. When the Maharishi refused to go on, the show was called off and more than half the tour dates were also subsequently cancelled.

America's first-ever National Basketball Association (NBA) championship took place in Pittsburgh on May 4, with the home-team Pipers beating the New Orleans Buccaneers 122-113. A week later, up-and-coming British singer Reg Dwight left the band Bluesology to pursue a solo career – and opted for a new name. Inspired by saxophone player Elton Dean and singer Long John Baldry, he chose to be known in future as Elton John – adding the middle name Hercules some years later.

Two of Britain's most notorious villains, Reggie and Ronnie Kray, were finally arrested on May 8 in a series of dawn raids across London's East End. Charged with murder, fraud, blackmail and assault, the Kray twins were both sentenced to life imprisonment in 1969, while their elder brother, Charlie, was given ten years for helping dispose of a body.

A couple of days later, emissaries from North Vietnam and the USA sat round the table in Paris for the first round of peace talks to end

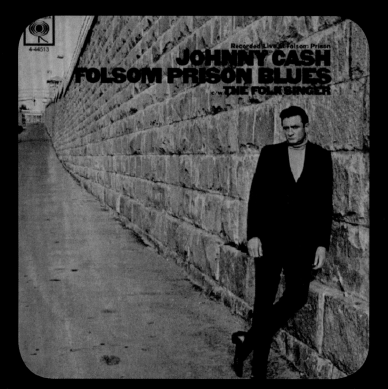

Left: Johnny Cash recorded his award winning album Folsom Prison Blues in the Californian state prison.

Opposite above: A business meeting at the offices of Apple with Paul McCartney (2ⁿᵈ left back) John Lennon (seated left) alongside PR man Derek Taylor and assistant Neil Aspinall.

Opposite below: Double world champion, Scottish racing driver Jim Clark was killed in April.

the Vietnam War. It had taken six days for the parties to decide on the venue for the talks, which would go on for another four years.

Founding member of the Rolling Stones, Brian Jones, made what would be his last appearance with the band at the *New Musical Express* Poll Winners Concert at Wembley Pool on Sunday, May 12. Returning to the stage after an absence of over a year, the Stones performed their new single, 'Jumpin' Jack Flash', in front of 10,000 fans, who also saw Status Quo, Cliff Richard, Amen Corner, The Move, Dusty Springfield and Scott Walker.

For the *NME*'s rival paper, *Melody Maker*, the Stones' new single was the record that would "prove one way or another whether they are still a major chart force", reckoning, "They've got a No.1 with this, the most commercial Stones single in a long, long time."

In the world of football, Manchester City pipped rivals Manchester United to the First Division title by just two points, while West Bromwich Albion beat Everton 1-0 after extra time in the FA Cup Final. However, the month and the season ended on a major high for Manchester United, when they became the first

APRIL NUMBER ONES

SINGLES

'What a Wonderful World' –
Louis Armstrong (UK)
'Young Girl' – Gary Puckett &
The Union Gap (UK)
'Honey' – Bobby Goldsboro (US)
'Tighten Up' – Archie Bell & The Drells (US)

ALBUMS

John Wesley Harding – Bob Dylan (UK)
Scott 2 – Scott Walker (UK)
The Graduate – Soundtrack (US)
Bookends – Simon & Garfunkel (US)

English team to win the European Cup, beating Portugese champions Benfica 4-1 after extra time at Wembley Stadium.

The 21-storey Ronan Point tower block of flats in Canning Town East London partially collapsed on May 16 following a gas explosion, killing four people. It had only been open two months, and was eventually demolished in 1986.

The civil war between Nigerian government forces and the state of Biafra, which began in 1967, became a humanitarian tragedy this month with the people of Biafra suffering a major famine. Estimates in 1968 put the death total at 3 million, including close to two million who had died from starvation. The war finally ended in 1970 when Biafran forces were forced to surrender to the Nigerian army.

Left: Thousands of people took to the streets of Paris in May to protest against the government of President Charles De Gaulle.

GOUVERNEMENT POPULAIRE
...DIANTS AUX COTES DE LA CLASSE OUVRIÈRE

...NION DES ÉTUDIANTS COMMUNISTES

UNWRAPPING APPLE RECORDS

Although The Beatles launched a number of Apple companies during 1967 – Apple Boutique, Apple Films, Apple Publishing and Apple Electronics – it wasn't until January 1968 that they formally agreed to change the name of their company from Beatles Ltd. to Apple Corps.

In May, Lennon and McCartney travelled to New York and announced to the world the formation of the business that made most sense – Apple Records. Appearing on NBC's *The Tonight Show* with guest host Joe Garagiola sitting in for Johnny Carson, they explained their thinking.

"We decided to play businessmen for a bit because we've got to run our own affairs now," said Lennon, adding, "We've got this thing called Apple which is going to be records, films and electronics. That's the idea. We'll find out what happens."

Three months later, on August 30, the first records to be issued by Apple and bearing the new apple logo hit the shops. The Beatles 'Hey Jude' was first but, as the group were still signed to EMI/Parlophone, the record carried the prefix R5722. On the same day, Mary Hopkin's 'Those Were The Days' (prefix Apple 2) came out, and was followed on September 6 by Jackie Lomax's 'Sour Milk Sea' (Apple 3) and 'Thinggumybob' by The Black Dyke Mills Band (Apple 4).

Apart from 'Hey Jude', only Hopkin's single made any sort of impression, reaching No. 1 in the UK and No. 2 in the US, but Apple Records was in business. Over the next eight years, the individual Beatles plus artists such as James Taylor, Hot Chocolate, Badfinger and Billy Preston all released records on the Apple label.

One act who wanted to be on The Beatles' record label but never managed it was Crosby Stills and Nash, as Graham Nash explained. "We really had our hearts set on Apple Records. It was a happening label." However, as the former singer with the Hollies added, even an audition for George Harrison and Peter Asher (the label's A&R chief) failed to impress: "I could see on their faces the effect we had. Or so I thought. A few days later we got a formal reply: 'Not for us.' Turns out they didn't hear it at all."

However, running their own business was not a natural fit for The Beatles, and by 1970 the company seemingly existed only to collect the group's royalty cheques. Nonetheless, McCartney told *Rolling Stone* magazine in 1974, "I think the Apple thing was great," although he also added, "The main downfall was that we were less businessmen and more heads, which was very pleasant and enjoyable. We got a man in who started to say 'come on, sign it all over to me' which was a fatal mistake."

Others were also sceptical about The Beatles business plans. Photographer Gered Mankowitz watched from the sidelines and observed, "They weren't business people, and they wanted to be patrons of artists that were of interest to them. It was all pretty stoned hippy and lovely for a few minutes, and then somebody pointed out that it was a business."

From the earliest days, journalist Mick Brown could see what lay ahead for Apple. "It was always destined to be madness. It was driven by a great degree of idealism; they saw it as a way of offering people – poets, inventors, artists – a way to come forward. But of course they were completely naïve, and had no idea of how much money they had and no idea of how much they were spending."

Above: Mama Cass went solo and hit the charts with 'Dream A Little Dream Of Me' in August.

Below: Skipper Bobby Charlton holds the European Cup aloft after Manchester United's victory over Portugese champions Benfica.

JUNE

JUNE NUMBER ONES

SINGLES

'Young Girl' – Gary Puckett & The Union Gap (UK
'Jumpin' Jack Flash' – Rolling Stones (UK)
'Mrs Robinson' – Simon & Garfunkel (US)
'This Guy's in Love with You' – Herb Alpert (US)

ALBUMS

John Wesley Harding – Bob Dylan (UK)
Love Andy – Andy Williams (UK) / *Dock of the
Bay* – Otis Redding (UK)
Ogden's Nut Gone Flake – Small Faces (UK)
Bookends – Simon & Garfunkel (US)

The world's leading pop artist Andy Warhol was shot and wounded in New York on June 3, when American radical feminist Valerie Solanas attacked him as he entered his Factory studio. Later diagnosed as suffering from paranoid schizophrenia, Solanas, who had worked on Warhol's films, was sentenced to three years in prison, and died in 1988.

In the same week, up-and-coming Canadian folk singer Joni Mitchell made her debut in Los Angeles with a week of gigs at the Troubador club. She was promoting her eponymous first album, which was produced by David Crosby,

with Stephen Still on bass, and peaked at No. 189 on the US album chart.

In a dispute over equal pay, 187 female machinists at the Ford Motor Company's plant in Dagenham, East London went on strike on June 7 and brought car production to a halt. They were joined by machinists at the company's Merseyside operation in Halewood, and it was three weeks before they returned to work. The action eventually led to the Equal Pay Act of 1970, and was captured in the successful 2010 film *Made in Dagenham*.

Italy became European football champions

when they beat Yugoslavia 1-0 in the final in Rome on June 10. Just four teams from the qualifying rounds went to Italy, with World Champions England losing to Yugoslavia in their semi-final. However, thanks to goals from Bobby Charlton and Geoff Hurst, they beat the Soviet Union 2-0 in the third place play-off.

Left: Pierre Trudeau topped the Canadian elections to become Prime Minister in 1968 and introduced the country to 'Trudeauism'.

Above: Senator Robert F Kennedy with his wife Ethel in Los Angeles on the night he was assassinated in June 1968.

Two days later, Roman Polanski's film version of Ira Levin's book *Rosemary's Baby* premiered in America, with Mia Farrow and John Cassavettes in the lead roles – although it was Ruth Gordon who won an Oscar for Best Supporting Actress.

Hitmakers Manfred Mann were forced to delay the American release of their new single, 'My Name Is Jack', following a complaint from their US record company that a phrase ("super spade") in the song, written by John Simon, might "antagonize race relations." The band re-recorded the single and changed the potentially offensive words to "superman", but the record still sank without trace in America, while it reached No. 8 in the UK.

The man voted Britain's favourite comedian was found dead on June 24 in a flat in Sydney, Australia, where he was making a TV series. Tony Hancock was 44 years of age when he committed suicide after a glittering but troubled career, which included over 100 episodes of the BBC radio show *Hancock's Half Hour* from 1954. The show switched to television in 1956, and Hancock became the first artist to receive £1,000 for a 30-minute show.

On the afternoon of Saturday, May 29 Pink Floyd topped the bill at Britain's first-ever large-scale free concert held in London's Hyde Park. They were joined by Jethro Tull, Roy Harper and Tyrannosaurus Rex (led by 20-year-old Marc Bolan), and watched by over 15,000 fans. Disc jockey John Peel commented that it was "the nicest concert I've ever been to," while Floyd's Nick Mason said," This was a marvellous event... everyone seemed to be in the same good mood." Weirdly, *MM* reportedly fielded a number of calls from readers wanting to know how much it would cost to get in to the "free" show.

The month ended with US aircraft makers Lockheed introducing their giant C-5 Galaxy military-transport aircraft. One of the largest military airplanes in the world, it went into service with the US Air Force in 1969 and flew for another forty years.

SMALL FACES GO ROUND

Steve Marriott, Ronnie Lane, Kenny Jones and Ian McLagan made history for their band the Small Faces when they released their third album in a revolutionary round record sleeve.

Ogden's Nut Gone Flake featured the London-based group starting side one with a collection of seven self-composed songs, and then turning to comedian and actor Stanley Unwin – famous for his unique brand of gobbledygook language known as "Unwinese" – to act as narrator on side two.

In the words of *NME* reviewer Keith Altham, the album represented "the first real attempt at a musical, space-age fairy tale", while he quotes Unwin as suggesting that the whole thing is "a storm braining electrilode of the highest tudeimagnus."

Considered by some to be a "psychedelic masterpiece" which combined "trippy R&B and cockney charm", *Ogden's Nut Gone Flake* reached No. 1 the British album chart in June and stayed there for six weeks. It made no impression in America, although the band's single 'Itchycoo Park' had hit the US top twenty in 1967.

Even though the band refused to feature tracks from *Ogden's Nut Gone Flake* in their live shows, the album had made its mark by virtue of the unique design of the record sleeve, which represented the lid of a tobacco tin.

Gered Mankowitz had regularly photographed the Small Faces, through his association with their manager Andrew Loog Oldham and his Immediate record label. "I was very involved in that cover as I did all the photography and worked very closely with Sean Kenny, the famous set designer who was involved in the early planning," recalls Mankowitz, who suggests that the concept for the round cover came from the band members.

As the album itself contains no credits at all – not for performers, producer, engineer, writers, photographer or designers – it's difficult to confirm who did what, although Nick Tweddell and Pete Brown, two art-school friends of McLagan, were responsible for the cover illustration, and Mankowitz believes the Immediate in-house art department prepared the final artwork.

The round lid of the tin opened first, revealing tobacco and a packet of cigarette papers before folding out to show four separate photographs of the band members, and a final opening brought you to the record itself. "I photographed each of the Faces individually with one of them in the foreground and others in background in four locations – Steve Marriott is in his flat, Ronnie Lane is in his flat, Ian McLagan was in my studio and Kenny Jones was somewhere out in the country, " explains Mankowitz.

"It was a fabulous idea but it wasn't practical – the albums rolled off the shelves but it was a lovely thing to be associated with, and it was very much in keeping with the spirit and energy of Immediate – and it cost a fortune."

Talking after the album's release, Steve Marriott said, "Out biggest hang-up now may be trying to follow an album like *Ogden's Nut Gone Flake*. If the next one doesn't go to No. 1 people will start crowing that it's not as good as the last one." He needn't have worried, because there wouldn't be a "next one" – he left the group in January 1969 to form Humble Pie.

DAILY NEWS

NEW YORK'S PICTURE NEWSPAPER ®

8¢

10¢ OUTSIDE L.I. AND SUBURBS

Vol. 49. No. 296   Copr. 1968 News Syndicate Co. Inc.   New York, N.Y. 10017, Tuesday, June 4, 1968*   WEATHER: Sunny and warm.

ACTRESS SHOOTS ANDY WARHOL

Cries 'He Controlled My Life'

NEWS photo by Jack Smith

Guest From London Shot With Pop Art Movie Man

Shot in attack on underground movie producer Andy Warhol, London art gallery owner Mario Amaya, about 30, walks to ambulance. Warhol was shot and critically wounded by one of his female stars, Valerie Solanas, 28, the "girl on the staircase" in one of his recent films. She walked into Andy's sixth-floor office at 33 Union Square West late yesterday afternoon and got off at least five shots. Valerie later surrendered. See ➞ —*Stories on page 3*

NEWS photo by Tom Monaster

Warhol (r.) was doing his thing with friend in Village spot recently.

BORN
Australian singer/actor Jason Donovan (1)
British singer David Gray (13)
Italian football legend Paolo Maldini (26)

DIED
Blind author and activist Helen Keller (1)
Randolph Churchill, politician son
of Sir Winston Churchill (6)
American jazz guitarist Wes Montgomery (15)

Left: The attempted murder of pop artist Andy Warhol in New York made headline news in June 1968.

Above: Soul singer Aretha Franklin hit the top ten with 'Say A Little Prayer'.

"Rock music became the lingua franca for young people […] and musicians did carry the protest message"

Mick Brown

Left: Over 50,000 people gathered on the streets of Washington DC in June as part of the Poor People's March.

Above: Influential hard rock band Iron Butterfly scored a big hit with their psychedelic opus, 'In-A-Gadda-Da-Vida'.

JULY

The month opened with Bob Dylan's backing group The Band, who as The Hawks had been heavily criticized when they played on his early "electric" tours, releasing their debut album, *Music From Big Pink*, which peaked at No. 30 in America. The title was taken from the pink house in New York State where the band had been living and working with Dylan.

British yachtsman Alec Rose returned to Portsmouth harbour on July 3 after his 354-day solo round the world trip in his yacht *Lively Lady*. He was greeted by thousands of well-wishers and was knighted later in the month.

Saddam Hussein, who would take over as President of Iraq in 1979 and lead his country into war against Allied western forces, was named Vice Chairman of the Revolutionary Council on July 17 following the "July Revolution", a coup d'état that saw the Arab Socialist Ba'ath Party gain power.

Beatle George Harrison broke a long silence to tell the UK's music press what the group had been doing since returning from India. "It appears we are doing less, but we're doing more but the public don't see it. When we toured we were seen on stage, and getting on and off aeroplanes. Now we do our work in private, in offices and studios." He also confirmed, "I'm still meditating and I'm still a vegetarian. No I'm not in touch with the Maharishi."

An emerging English four-piece group called The Nice led by keyboard showman Keith Emerson found themselves in the midst of a major row when it came to promoting their single 'America', an arrangement of Leonard Bernstein's piece from the musical *West Side Story*. The advertising poster featured the group with the faces of the assassinated John

F Kennedy, Robert Kennedy and Martin Luther King superimposed on children's heads. The record was banned in America, and the poster was withdrawn in the UK after record stores shunned the record and promoters refused to book the band.

Meanwhile over in California, the influential semi-conductor technology company Intel was born when Gordon E Moore and Robert Noyce created a business called NM Electronics, which they quickly re-named Intel – from Integrated Electronics.

Above: The Teddington Studios of Thames Television, which began transmitting in July 1968.

Right: British singing star Tom Jones entertained Elvis Presley and topped the UK album chart with *Delilah*.

July 20 was the day when the world's first Special Olympics summer games took place in Chicago's Soldier Field. The one-day event, sponsored to the tune of $25,000 by the Kennedy Foundation, featured 1,000 athletes with intellectual disabilities. Three days later, baseball star Hank Aaron of the Atlanta Braves hit his 500th home run – in pursuit of Babe Ruth's 30-year-old record of 714. Aaron would eventually pass Ruth's total in 1974.

The month ended with two memorable television moments. Thames Television – there was a plan to call it Tower Television – began transmitting in the London region from Monday until 7pm on Friday, when London Weekend Television took over. The next day – on July 31 – the BBC broadcast the first episode of the comedy show *Dad's Army*. Written by Jimmy Perry and David Croft and starring Arthur Lowe, it ran for 80 episodes until 1977 and in 2004 was voted fourth-best British sitcom.

BORN
YouTube CEO Susan Wojcicki (5)
Jorja Fox, *CIS* TV series actress (7)
Manic Street Preachers drummer Sean Moore (30)

DIED
Putlitzer Prize for Music winner Leo Sowerby (7)
Anglo-German actress Lilian Harvey (27)
Charles Mayo medical practitioner/
founder of Mayo Clinic (28)

JULY NUMBER ONES

SINGLES
'Baby Come Back' – The Equals (UK)
'I Pretend' – Des O'Connor (UK)
'Mony Mony' – Tommy James & the Shondells (UK)
'This Guy's in Love with You' – Herb Alpert (US)
'Grazing in the Grass' – Hugh Masakela (US)

ALBUMS
Ogden's Nut Gone Flake – Small Faces (UK);
Bookends – Simon & Garfunkel (US)
Beat of the Brass – Herb Alpert & the
Tijuana Brass (US)

Previous pages: Cream – one of the first super groups – played two farewell concerts at London's Royal Albert Hall before Eric Clapton (left), Ginger Baker (centre) and Jack Bruce split up and went their separate ways.

Left: Integrated Electronics became technology giants Intel under the guidance of co-founder Gordon Moore.

YELLOW SUBMARINE

When Brian Epstein died suddenly in August 1967, he left The Beatles a host of business issues to sort out. One of them was the subject of a third film for United Artists, who had released *A Hard Day's Night* and *Help* – "It was the third movie that we owed United Artists," explained Lennon. "Brian had set it up, and we had nothing to do with it."

Faced with this situation, The Beatles gave their support to the creation of a full-length cartoon, which involved 40 animators and artists. The idea came from a series of Beatles' cartoon films broadcast on American television from 1965 to 1967. They were made by New York writer and producer Al Brodax, who persuaded Epstein to agree to the feature film, and for the group to supply some new songs for the cartoon.

The final script for *Yellow Submarine* included contributions from the Scaffold's Roger McGough (who was apparently paid but un-credited) alongside the official writing team of Brodax, Lee Minoff, John Mendelsohn and Eric Segal, while producer Brodax hired Canadian animator George Dunning as the director.

The film featured actors as the voices of the four Beatles alongside popular performers such as Dick Emery and Lance Percival, and respected film critic Alexander Walker wrote, "*Yellow Submarine* is the key film of the Beatles. It's a trip through the contemporary mythology that the quartet from Merseyside has helped to create."

The film premiered at the London Pavilion in July 1968, where the Beatles were joined by musicians Donovan, Sandie Shaw, PJ Proby, Mick Jagger and Alan Price plus model Twiggy and disc jockeys Simon Dee and Tony Blackburn.

While Lennon admitted, "I liked the movie, the artwork," and Starr added, "I thought it was really innovative with great animation," there were those who were less impressed. *NME*'s Andy Gray described it as "colourful, sometimes ingenious but overall rather boring."

For professional artist Lynne Timington, "It was kinda disappointing because it was a cartoon and we thought it was going to be another *Magical Mystery Tour*. I was excited about it, but then it came out and I didn't really get it. It didn't ever grab me and I've never gone back to it."

Photographer Gered Mankowitz wasn't totally convinced either. "I did go and see it and was probably quite stoned in the front row of a cinema somewhere. However weird some of the images were, it just seemed like a commercial showbizzy thing to do. I don't think we sat around and thought this was really out there, but we did admire the scale of The Beatles."

On the other hand, for future music executive Jonathan Morrish, it was anything but a disappointment: "I was baffled by it all, bamboozled – it is the most astonishing piece of work. I love it, it is genius, it is astonishing even though the music isn't great." *MM*'s Chris Welch was another big fan, and he wrote in 1968, "The cartoon is the most imaginative, advanced and entertaining since [the Walt Disney classic] *Fantasia*."

Even though they had little involvement in the creation of the film – and only supplied four songs for the soundtrack – The Beatles did agree to make a brief appearance at the end of the film, which, surprisingly, was never put on general release in the UK.

Yellow Submarine opened in America in the autumn of 1968 and was a major box-office hit, playing to full houses across the country, and the subsequent soundtrack album, released in 1969, reached the top three in both the UK and US.

AUGUST

A year after the launch of Radio 1, the BBC station controller Robin Scott replied to a letter from a reader in *MM* and explained why they only employed male presenters. "Women do not take to girl deejays," he said before adding, "But we are always ready to listen to approaches from girls." It would be another year before Annie Nightingale became the station's first female disc jockey, in October 1969.

In another music-related story, it was reported in *The Times* that Britain's pop charts were set for a shake-up, with the British Market Research Bureau taking over compiling the weekly singles and album charts from sales diaries submitted by 300 shops. The final charts would then be calculated by a computer, with the new system set to start in November. The UK singles chart had been introduced in 1952, with an album chart starting four years later.

At America's Republican Party convention in Miami, Richard M Nixon emerged as the party's nomination for the November Presidential election. The campaign by the former Vice-President, who lost to John F Kennedy in the 1960 election, included an in-car rubbish bag with the slogan "America Needs NIXON! This Time" and the message "Vote like your whole world depended on it."

In their August 10 issue, *MM* reviewed new albums by two of Britain's best known bands – Pink Floyd and The Moody Blues. While accepting that Floyd's music could "just as easily antagonize as satisfy," they suggested that on *A Saucerful of Secrets* they "have not eschewed rhythm, and excitement" and urged readers to "give the Floyd a listen – it isn't really so painful." Considering The Moody Blues' *In Search of the Lost Chord*, complete with

AUGUST NUMBER ONES

SINGLES

'Mony Mony' – Tommy James &
the Shondells (UK)

'Fire' – Crazy World of Arthur Brown (UK)

'Do It Again' – Beach Boys (UK)

'Hello, I Love You' – The Doors (US)

'People Got to Be Free' – The Rascals (US)

ALBUMS

Ogden's Nut Gone Flake – Small Faces (UK)

Delilah – Tom Jones (UK)

Bookends – Simon & Garfunkel (UK)

Beat of the Brass – Herb Alpert &
the Tijuana Brass (US)

Wheels of Fire – Cream (US)

POP ON THE ISLE OF WIGHT

Forever known as the Isle of Wight festival, the first pop event to take place on the small island off the south coast of England was actually billed as the Great South Coast Bank Holiday Pop Festivity, and took place on August 31.

It was held in a 40-acre field near Godshill, owned by farmers Ray and Ron Foulk who organized it as a fund-raiser for a local swimming pool. The festival started at 6pm on Saturday and ran through until 10am the next day and the 10,000 fans were treated to sets by the American band Jefferson Airplane plus The Move, Fairport Convention, The Pretty Things, Tyrannosaurus Rex and assorted acts such as Hunter's Musket, Mirage and Harsh Reality – all introduced by John Peel.

Arthur Brown – he of the Crazy World – was forced to abandon his plan to arrive by balloon due to high winds, which also meant he wasn't able to set fire to his famous headgear. *NME's* reporter on the spot was also less than impressed with the event, which he described as "16 hours of make-do, make-shift and hasty improvisation." Bands were required to play on a stage made up of two trailers covered by scaffolding and canvas, and The Move's manager considered the event to be "a great louse-up."

While fans had to put up with poor transport links and 30-minute breaks between sets, the organizers and local sponsors quickly disassociated themselves with anything that happened "on the night." The local National Farmers' Union raised concerns for the wellbeing of nearby livestock, and the island's Magistrates objected to the organizers advertising bars before they had even applied for a drinks licence

Confirming that Jefferson Airplane – who arrived with 30 lighting and sound technicians and five tons of equipment – were given "easily the best reception of any of the 14 acts", the *NME* concluded that, despite all police leave being cancelled, the only trouble came from some burnt-out chairs, and the only casualties "were those who were treated for exposure."

poems and a mantra, the reviewer wrote, "Great music but we'd hate to see the Moodies take themselves too seriously."

Britain's last steam-train passenger service set out on August 11 with a trip from Liverpool to Carlisle and back. Costing 15 guineas (£15.75p), the trip – which was dubbed the "fifteen guinea special" – arrived 33 minutes late in Carlisle, but was just nine minutes late on the return journey to Liverpool.

On August 21 the US Medal of Honour – or the Congressional Medal – was awarded posthumously to Rifleman James Anderson Jnr, who became the first black man to receive America's highest military decoration. The citation read that Anderson, who was killed in Vietnam on February 28, 1967, displayed "conspicuous gallantry."

France became the fourth country to join the nuclear arms race when they exploded their

first hydrogen bomb – codename Canopus – in the Pacific on August 24. They joined the US, U.S.S.R. and UK as nuclear nations just ahead of China.

Two months after their appearance in Hyde Park with Pink Floyd, Tyrannosaurus Rex found themselves in the UK album chart with their debut offering *My People Were Fair and Had Sky in Their Hair... But Now They're Content to Wears Stars on Their Brow*, which, surprisingly, never made it as the world's longest album title

– check out Chumbawamba for that honour. Marc Bolan and partner Steve Peregrine Took, who answered an advert seeking "other astral flyers like with cars, amplification and that which never grows in window boxes" peaked at No. 15 with their first album.

Left: Scottish singer Donovan travelled to India and hit the charts in the US and UK during 1968

Left: The members of Pink Floyd take part in a very literal photo shoot in Los Angeles.

Above: Music festival fever spread across the globe, including to Rome, where the famed Baths of Caracalla hosted a two-day extravaganza.

Right: France became the fourth nuclear nation in August following H-bomb tests over Murora in the Pacific Ocean.

BORN
Marine Le Pen, leader of France's
National Front Party (5)
American X-Files star Gillian Anderson (9)
British record breaking cyclist Chris Boardman (26)

DIED
Pulitzer prize-winning writer Esther Forbes (12)
Australian test cricketer Stan McCabe (25)
Princess Marina of Greece/Denmark
and Duchess of Kent (27)

SEPTEMBER

Japanese carmaker Nissan, which launched its first car in 1914, started to sell its Datsun-model cars in Britain for the first time, and reached the 6,000 sales mark in three years. A day later, on June 2, over 11,000 people were killed in Iran by two major earthquakes, which reached 7.4 on the Richter scale.

The Rolling Stones found themselves in trouble in America when radio stations banned their single 'Street Fighting Man' on the grounds that it might incite riots throughout the US. Commenting on the idea that the record was subversive, Mick Jagger replied, "Of course it's subversive. It's stupid to think that you can start a revolution with a record. I wish I could." He added, "The last time they banned one of our records in America it sold a million," but he was not so lucky this time as 'Street Fighting Man' just about made the US top 50.

Over 150 women – members of the New York Radical Women movement – protested against the Miss America pageant being held in Atlantic City on September 6. While Miss Illinois (Judith Ford) was declared the winner, the protesters compared the whole event to a country fair and crowned a sheep as Miss America.

Two of America's biggest new groups shared the bill at London's Roundhouse in the first week of the month. The Doors – with their single 'Hello, I Love You' at No. 1 in the US – supported Jefferson Airplane, while Big Brother & The Holding Company's second album, *Cheap Thrills*, was released to a review from *NME* that described the band as "a raving, screeching, noisy group" and lead singer Janis Joplin as "a sort of Shirley Bassey out of control." Originally called *Dope, Sex And Cheap Thrills*, the title was shortened by the band's record company to

Cheap Thrills, but it didn't stop it topping the US chart for eight weeks.

Tennis star Arthur Ashe became the first African-American man to win the US Open championship in New York on September 9. As he was an amateur, Ashe was not allowed to take the $14,000 first prize – which went to runner-up Tom Okker – while Britain's Virginia Wade took the ladies title, and $6000, the day before.

The largest-ever company merger in British history took place on June 13 when the General Electric Company (GEC) joined forces with English Electric to create an operation employing 250,000 people.

Three days later, the Post Office introduced first-class and second-class postal services costing 5d (approx. 2.5p) and 4d (2p), with the intention of raising an extra £25 million.

BORN
British film director Guy Ritchie (10)
American actor Will Smith (25)
Bros members Luke & Matt Goss (29)

DIED
Karl Rankl Austrian composer/conductor (6)
Scottish/American golfer Tommy Armour (11)
Rock 'n' roll deejay Dewey Philips (28)

SEPTEMBER NUMBER ONES

SINGLES
'I've Gotta get a Message to You' –
The Bee Gees (UK)
'Hey Jude' – The Beatles (UK)
'Those Were the Days' – Mary Hopkin (UK)
'People Got to Be Free' – The Rascals (US)
'Harper Valley P.T.A.' – Jeannie C Riley (US)
'Hey Jude' – The Beatles (US)

ALBUMS
Bookends – Simon & Garfunkel (UK)
Delilah – Tom Jones (UK)
Wheels of Fire – Cream (US)
Waiting for the Sun – The Doors (US)
Time Peace/Greatest Hits – The Rascals (US)

A cricket tour of South Africa by England was called off by the MCC, the former governing body of cricket in the UK, when the South African authorities refused to accept the presence of Cape Coloured cricketer Basil D'Oliveira in the English team. Having left South Africa in 1960, D'Oliveira was qualified to play for England, and

Right: Traffic Jam changed their name to Status Quo and released their debut hit Pictures Of Matchstick Men.

Left: Jimi Hendrix (centre) and The Experience – Noel Redding (l) and Mitch Mitchell – topped the US charts while there album was banned in the UK.

Below: American chainsaw entrepreneur Robert P McCulloch paid £1 million for London Bridge.

Right: Jack Lord, star of the long-running US TV crime series *Hawaii Five-O* which began in September 1968.

the affair led to South Africa and its apartheid regime becoming isolated with no official visiting sporting tours until 1990.

CBS TV in America launched the police series *Hawaii Five-O* on September 20 and the show, with Jack Lord, ran for an initial 12 seasons, and eventually became the longest-running crime show in television history until the arrival of *Law And Order*. In the same week, CBS also debuted its news magazine programme *60 Minutes*, which continues to this day and boasts amongst its original broadcasters the likes of Walter Cronkite and Dan Rather.

Spanish-born singer Placido Domingo – one of the celebrated "Three Tenors" alongside Luciano Pavarotti and Jose Carreras – made his debut at New York's Metropolitan Opera House on September 29, when he stood in for Franco Corelli in the opera *Adriano Lecouvreur*. On what would be the first of over 550 performances at the Met, the *New York Times* described Domingo as "a strapping fellow with a plangent and sizeable voice."

HEY JUDE/REVOLUTION

The Beatles returned to the top of the charts in both Britain and America in September 1968 – nine months after their previous chart topper – with 'Hey Jude', which racked up sales of over four million copies worldwide in just two months.

It was written in the main by McCartney, who had Lennon's son Julian in mind when he composed the song after the split between John and Cynthia Lennon. "I thought as a friend of the family I would motor out to Weybridge and tell them that everything was alright", said McCartney. "I had about an hour's drive. I would always turn the radio off and try to make up songs, just in case."

After he changed Jools to Jude – "I just thought a better name was Jude" – McCartney and his bandmates went into Abbey Road Studios, and Trident Studios in July and August, to complete recording.

Released worldwide on August 26, the record was a double first – the first record issued with the group's new Apple logo on the label, and The Beatles' longest-ever single at 7 minutes and 11 seconds. Producer George Martin believed that singles could not run for that long but, when he made his views known, he was "shouted down by the boys," with Lennon asking, "Why not?" The Beatles' producer added, "I couldn't think of an answer really – except the pathetic one that disc jockeys wouldn't play it. He [John] said, 'They will if it's us.'"

It was the UK's biggest-selling record of 1968, the group's 15th No. 1, and it remains the group's second-most-successful single ever with sales of over 10 million – just behind 'I Want To Hold Your Hand' with 12 million. To help sales, McCartney went along to the empty Apple shop in Baker Street and painted the titles of both sides of the single on the whitewashed windows.

Looking back at the record that almost bears his name, Julian Lennon said, "It has been an absolute honour to have someone, not only write a song about you, but especially Paul, and especially in that circumstance."

The reviews of the new Beatles' single were equally enthusiastic, although, interestingly, the Nice's Keith Emerson agreed with Martin in his Blind Date review in *MM*, saying, "I can see deejays dying to get in before the end." *NME*'s Derek Johnson described it as a "beautiful, compelling song", but he, too, had doubts about its "extreme length and 40-piece orchestra."

America's *Billboard* considered the record to be "a potent two-sided winner", and *NME*'s reviewer also picked up on the quality of the B-side, describing the lyrics of 'Revolution' as "thoughtful and highly topical." For Liz Woodcraft, 'Revolution' – with Lennon choosing to use the phrase "count me out" – brought back memories of her days at Birmingham University. "When we were sitting-in in autumn 1968, we also slept-in and we were in the great hall where there was a record player. We'd wake up every morning to someone playing 'Revolution', but I didn't like it because it actually had a fairly negative message about revolutions. I was hoping there would be a revolution of some sort but the words of the song say 'no, no, no'."

Almost twenty years, later the single version of 'Revolution' was the subject of a major legal wrangle when Apple sued Capitol Records in America and the Nike company, after the track was used in a 1987 TV commercial for sportswear.

Nike had paid $250,000 to Capitol and Michael Jackson (who by then owned the publishing rights) who had both given their permission, after Yoko Ono (on the basis that her late husband John Lennon had written 'Revolution') had given her blessing. Ten years on, George Harrison made clear his feelings about Ono's decision when he said, "Four of us were a partnership and it's daft when three people and the company are trying to set certain precedents and establish certain things and one of them is going off on the side and doing a deal. It makes everybody else look stupid."

Apple, who had never been consulted about the use of a Beatles track, sued for $15 million but Nike continued to run the commercial while the court case rumbled on, and in 1988 switched to using 'Instant Karma', which was owned by Ono. As a result, it was agreed that no Beatles recording of their songs would be used to sell any products, and it was left to Paul McCartney to explain, "The song was about revolution not bloody tennis shoes."

Left: American tennis star Arthur Ashe became the first – and, to date, only – black man to ever win the men's singles title at the US Open.

OCTOBER

BORN
Radiohead's Thom Yorke (7)
Australian actor Hugh Jackman (12)
Jamaican rapper Shaggy (22)

DIED
French artist Marcel Duchamp (2)
British music-hall star Bud Flanagan (20)

Left: 20 year-old Mexican athlete Norma de Soleto became the first woman to light the Olympic flame at the Mexico Olympic.

Right: American athletes Tommie Smith (centre) and John Carlos raised black-gloved fists on the victory podium in Mexico.

Two stories in the music papers in the first week of the month told readers that The Beatles had booked London's Royal Albert Hall for a live concert at the end of the year – claiming that Paul McCartney wanted to perform on stage again – while *The Sound of Music* was recognized as the best-selling album in British music history. The soundtrack album had passed the two million sales mark and spent 180 weeks in the *NME* top ten, and the paper calculated that, if all the copies the album sold in the UK were stacked together, they would reach 15 times the height of the Empire State Building.

At the same time, Britain got a new motorway link with the opening of the final 35-mile stage of the M1 – from Rotherham to Leeds – completing the road from London, which had been started in 1959.

Cult classic American horror movie *The Night of the Living Dead* premiered in Pittsburgh – where much of the movie was shot – on October 1. Directed, edited and co-written by George Romero, the film was made with a budget of just $114,000. And Jimi Hendrix produced and directed his Experience's album *Electric Ladyland*, which was dubbed a "mixed-up, muddled, mutinous and menacing two-album package" by the press, but still raced to No. 1 in America and reached the UK top ten, despite retailers refusing to stock the album because of the 19 naked ladies on the cover.

One of the earliest incidents in "the troubles" in Northern Ireland took place in Derry on October 5, when protesters defied a government order banning a civil-rights march and were confronted by police officers who injured over 100 people in a number of baton charges.

Defending baseball champions St Louis Cardinals lost a 3-1 series lead to eventually go down 4-3 to the Detroit Tigers in the best-of-seven World Series on October 10. While the Tigers' Denny McLain became the first pitcher to win 30 games in a season since 1934, blind Puerto Rican singer Jose Feliciano performed a controversial slow Latin-jazz version of the 'Star Spangled Banner' in the Tigers' stadium.

1

OCTOBER NUMBER ONES

SINGLES
'Those Were the Days' – Mary Hopkin (UK)
'Hey Jude' – The Beatles (US)

ALBUMS
Bookends – Simon & Garfunkel (UK)
Greatest Hits – The Hollies (UK)
Time Peace/Greatest Hits – The Rascals (US)
Cheap Thrills – Big Brother &
The Holding Company (US)

Defence announced that around 240,000 American troops – having served their mandatory one-year tour – were being sent back to Vietnam for an involuntary second mission because of "the length of the war."

Long jumper Bob Beamon broke all records when he covered 21 feet and ¾ inches (6.41 metres) at the Olympic Games in Mexico on October 18. The New York athlete's leap stood as the world record for 23 years, and it remains the Olympic long jump record.

When the police raided the flat where Lennon and Ono were living in Montagu Square in central London (previously occupied by Jimi Hendrix) on October 18, they found cannabis, and charged them both with obstructing the police in the execution of a search warrant. They appeared at Marylebone Magistrates Court the next day and were remanded on bail until

Left: Costing just $114,000 to make George Romero's *Night Of the Living Dead* became a cult horror movie following its opening in Pittsburgh.

Above: A sunrise over Florida was captured during one of Apollo 7's 163 orbits of the earth.

One day later the world awoke to see the first live television pictures sent from a manned orbiting American spacecraft. The Apollo 7 crew of Walter Schirra, Don Eisele and Walter Cunningham transmitted six broadcasts from their spacecraft during their 10-day flight and 163 orbits of the earth.

Six years after work started, London's rebuilt Euston station was officially opened by Queen Elizabeth II on October 14, and boasted 18 new platforms.

On the same day the US Department of

LAUNCHING LED ZEPPELIN

Following Keith Relf, Jim McCarty and Chris Dreja deciding to leave the hit-making band the Yardbirds, guitarist Jimmy Page was left with the problem of finding musicians for a new group.

The first person he recruited was bass player John Paul Jones – they were both regular session players and arrangers – before being recommended to see a Midlands-based singer named Robert Plant. The group's new singer, in turn, suggested drummer John Bonham to complete the line-up of the band, which Page named the New Yardbirds.

Talking to *MM* in October 1968, Page explained that forming the new group was not easy. "I thought I'd never get a band together. I've always shied of leadership in the past because of all that ego thing." He also announced plans for a first album and a US tour, and even picked out the venue for their UK debut – "I'm hoping the Marquee will be a good scene."

However, the New Yardbirds performed for the first time in Copenhagen on September 7, before making it to London for a UK debut at the famous club in London's Wardour Street on October 18. The following day, at Liverpool University, they played their last show as the New Yardbirds.

The Who's drummer, Keith Moon, had often used the phrase "going down like a lead Zeppelin" to describe a disastrous show, and Page had become a fan of the line but left out the "a" and re-named his band Led Zeppelin. They made their debut at the Battersea Park Road campus of Surrey University on Friday October 25, for what was billed as the "First Big Dance of the Term".

However, the change of name from New Yardbirds to Led Zeppelin didn't happen overnight, as a poster for their gig at the Roundhouse on November 9 still had the name Yardbirds (not even New) as top of the bill, but with the words "now known as Led Zeppelin" printed underneath.

Page's plan to tour America came to fruition in December when Led Zeppelin began a three-month trek in Denver, supporting Vanilla Fudge. Promoter Barry Fey later wrote about the band's US debut concert. "Robert Plant let it rip, and everyone in the audience was stunned. You didn't have to be a genius to know that Led Zeppelin was going to be a smash."

In 2004 – in the wake of his band selling close to 300 million records worldwide, including certified sales in America of 110 million – Jimmy Page was invited to unveil a plaque at Surry University commemorating Led Zeppelin's historic first gig back in October 1968.

November, when Lennon admitted possession of cannabis and was fined £150.

Former US First Lady Jacqueline Kennedy, the widow of President John F Kennedy, married Greek magnate Aristole Onassis on his private island of Skorpios on October 20. A couple of days later President Johnson signed into law America's 1968 Gun Control Act, which restricted firearms ownership, banned mail order sales of guns, and limited gun ownership in the case of felons and the mentally handicapped.

Motown star Marvin Gaye released 'I Heard It Through The Grapevine', and within a month his version of the Norman Whitfield and Barrett Strong song went to No. 1 in America – and stayed there for seven weeks. It became the biggest-selling record in Motown's history, and eventually made it to No. 1 in the UK in early 1969.

On the final day of the month, American President Johnson announced in a radio broadcast to the nation that he was ordering the end of "all air, naval and artillery bombardment of North Vietnam." With the peace talks continuing in Paris, Johnson told America's citizens that he had reached the decision "in the belief that this action can lead to progress toward a peaceful settlement of the Vietnam War."

Above: Aristotle Onassis (l) with former US first lady Jackie Kennedy and her daughter Caroline Kennedy.

Below: Dick Fosbury caused a sensation when he 'flopped' over the high jump bar to win gold at the Mexico Olympics.

NOVEMBER

Republican Richard M Nixon became the 37th President of the USA when he won the November 5 election against Democrat candidate Hubert Humphrey and the American Independent Party's George C Wallace. Winning 32 states and 43.4% of the vote – Humphrey took 42.7% – Nixon was expected to end the Vietnam War, as Woodcraft recalls. "I don't think there was a great ray of hope when Nixon came in although he had to end the War as nobody wanted it – there were too many body bags coming back."

Left: Grosvenor Square is engulfed by anti-war protestors looking to make a point to the American embassy.

Below: America's 37th President Richard Nixon and his wife Pat with their family after his victory over Democratic candidate Hubert Humphrey.

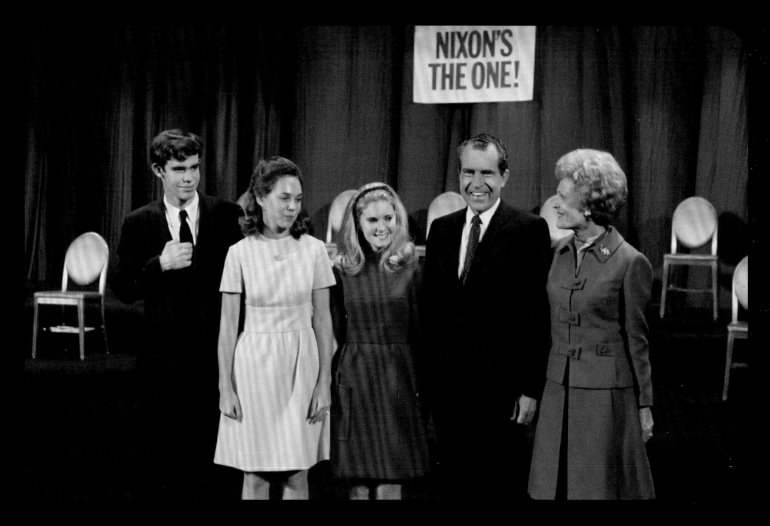

Three days later, "Great Train Robber" Bruce Reynolds, who had led the 15-strong gang who stole £2.6 million from a train in 1963, was reported to have been captured in a house in Torquay. The London-born career criminal had fled to Mexico after the robbery, and moved on to Canada and France before returning to Britain under the name Keith Hiller.

Over 250 years after it was founded, Yale University announced on November 14 that it would admit female students. The Connecticut-based college – the third-oldest higher-education institute in America – finally opened its doors to women in January 1969 with 576 women joining 4,000 men on the campus.

History was made on American television on November 22 when the first interracial kiss was aired in the sci-fi series *Star Trek*. In the episode "Plato's Stepchildren" – the 12th in the show's third season on NBC – Captain James Kirk (William Shatner) shared a kiss with Lieutenant Uhuru, played by African-American actress Nichelle Nichols.

The price of an album in the UK increased in late November following Labour's Chancellor of the Exchequer Roy Jenkins announcing, in the midst of a sterling crisis, an increase in purchase tax – the forerunner of VAT. The 5% increase to 55% put the cost of one particular double album up to over £3 .14s (£3.70p) from £3.13s (£3.65p).

British supergroup Cream – Eric Clapton, Jack Bruce and Ginger Baker – played what was announced as their final shows at London's Royal Albert Hall in front of 10,000 fans during the last week of the month. The group had been formed in 1966 and, during two years together, produced four hit singles and three UK and US hit albums, including the American No. 1 *Wheels of Fire*.

A new Race Relations Act came into effect in the UK on November 26, which made it illegal to refuse housing, employment or public services to people on the grounds of ethnic background. Labour Home Secretary James Callaghan told Parliament, "The House has rarely faced an issue of greater social significance for our country or

GEORGE AND JOHN GO SOLO

While Paul McCartney was probably the first Beatle to go solo when he wrote music for the 1966 film *The Family Way,* and was credited as a solo composer along with George Martin as his arranger, the first genuine solo album from the group came on November 1 with the release of George Harrison's *Wonderwall Music.*

It was also the soundtrack to the psychedelic film *Wonderwall,* directed by Joe Massot and starring Jane Birki, but Harrison's work became famous for being the first album released on the Apple label with the number SAPCOR 1. Featuring musicians from Liverpool band the Remo Four, including pianist Tony Ashton, recording began in Abbey Road in November 1967 and continued in India in January 1968, when Harrison teamed up with local Indian musicians in EMI's Bombay studios.

Explaining that the studio had no soundproofing, Harrison said, "If you listen closely to some of the Indian tracks on the LP you can hear taxis going by. They only had a big old EMI mono machine. It was incredible, I mixed everything as we did it."

The collection of rock, experimental and Indian music was greeted with mixed reviews, with *Record World* in America describing it as "moody and pretty" while the *Guardian* wrote that the individual members of the group had "musical ideas which cannot be related to the Beatles."

With limited advertising in the UK – there were just quarter-page adverts in the music press – the album failed to chart, but reached No. 49 in the US where full-page adverts appeared in *Billboard* and other magazines in advance of the film's opening in January 1969.

Just over a week after Harrison's album appeared, John Lennon, together with Yoko Ono and the Ono Band, issued his debut solo offering, entitled *Unfinished Music No. 1 – Two Virgins,* in America, and in the UK at the end of November, where it was numbered SAPCOR 2.

Recorded in the studio at his Kenwood home in Surrey, the album, according to Lennon, was a joint effort. He said, "She was doing her funny voice and I was pushing all the different buttons on my tape recorder getting sound effects." The end product was given just 1½ stars by *Rolling Stone* magazine, and only one star by *All Music,* and reportedly sold no more than 30,000 copies in total.

Evening Standard writer Ray Connolly wonders whether Epstein, if he had been alive, would have interfered with the release of the two solo efforts in the same month as a new Beatles album. "Maybe it wouldn't have happened with Epstein around, as he may have thought that putting out the Beatles would completely obliterate the other two – which it did anyway." In his review of Lennon and Ono's album, he wrote, "Very, very amusing, quite the best comedy record I've heard this year. In fact if you listen carefully you can hear Ms Ono doing her world famous impression of courting kangaroos... excellent Christmas party pantomime stuff for all the family."

However, the album's cover caused a media stir when it appeared with a nude photograph of Lennon and Ono, taken by Lennon in their London flat. After EMI refused to distribute the album in Britain, the independent Track Records (home to The Who) took over and put copies in a brown paper bag. It peaked at No. 149 in the US Top 200 album chart, although rare copies without a track listing but with wording on the front change hands for as much as £3,000.

our children." Less than a week later, a new Trade Descriptions Act was also introduced, which was intended to prevent shops and traders from describing goods in a misleading way.

After Madame Tussaud's waxworks in London had updated their Beatles models for the fifth time in four years, at a cost of over £8000, *NME* reported that plans for a series of live shows by The Beatles had once again been changed. Earlier in the month, it had been reported that the group were switching the venue from the Royal Albert Hall to the Chalk Farm Roundhouse for three shows in mid-December featuring Apple artists Jackie Lomax and Mary Hopkin.

Now it seemed fans would have to wait until after Christmas when the shows were reportedly going to take place in Liverpool, with The Beatles' PR man, Derek Taylor, telling the press, "It's likely we will be postponed until mid-January. But they will take place and that's a promise."

Above: The controversial inter-racial *Star Trek* kiss between William Shatner and Nichelle Nicholls.

Right: Demonstrators gather to protest against the 1968 Miss America pageant in Atlantic City

NOVEMBER NUMBER ONES

SINGLES

'With a Little Help from My Friends' –
Joe Cocker (UK)

'The Good, the Bad and the Ugly' –
Hugo Montenegro & His Orchestra (UK)

'Hey Jude' – The Beatles (US)

'Love Child' – Diana Ross & the Supremes (US)

ALBUMS

Greatest Hits – The Hollies (UK)

The Sound of Music – Soundtrack (UK)

Cheap Thrills – Big Brother &
The Holding Company (US)

Electric Ladyland – Jimi Hendrix Experience (US)

Left: Diana Ross with the Supremes topped the British album chart for the first time in 1968 with their *Greatest Hits* collection.

Above: Van Morrison left the group Them and released his critically acclaimed solo album *Astral Weeks* in July 1968.

DECEMBER

This is the Zodiac speaking. I am the murderer of the taxi driver over by Washington St + Maple St last night, to prove this here is a blood stained piece of his shirt. I am the same man who did in the people in the north bay a-rea. The S.F. Police could have caught me last night if they had

DECEMBER NUMBER ONES

SINGLES

'The Good, the Bad and the Ugly' –
Hugo Montenegro & His Orchestra (UK)
'Lily the Pink' – the Scaffold (UK)
'Love Child' – Diana Ross & the Supremes (US)
'I Heard It Through the Grapevine' –
Marvin Gaye (US)

ALBUMS

The Beatles – The Beatles (UK)
Wichita Lineman – Glen Campbell (US)
The Beatles – The Beatles (US)

After eight years away, Elvis Presley returned to the small screen when his NBC special *Singer Presents... Elvis* (often referred to as the '68 Comeback Special) was aired in the US on December 3. Recorded over two days back in June with backing musicians Scotty Moore, Charlie Hodge and D J Fontana, the 60-minute show was sponsored by Singer Sewing Machines, and *NME*'s American correspondent wrote, "Elvis at 33, with his weight tapered down and moving with all the sex that resulted in waist upward-only shots on the *Ed Sullivan Show* in 1956, is sensational."

Five months after their record company refused to release it, the Rolling Stones' album *Beggars Banquet* finally hit the shops on December 6 – in a plain white sleeve acting as the invitation to a banquet. The album was withdrawn by Decca back in July when they objected to the sleeve design featuring a graffiti-covered toilet with slogans such as "John Loves Yoko", "Mao Loves Lyndon" and "God Rolls His Own". Launched with a genuine banquet at the Queensgate Hotel in London, the album hit the top five on both sides of the Atlantic.

Later in the same week, The Stones gathered together at film studios in north London along with director Michael Lindsay-Hogg to film a television extravaganza called *The Rolling Stones' Rock 'n' Roll Circus*. With The Stones – including Mick Jagger as the ringmaster – were members of Fossett's Circus, plus the likes of The Who, Jethro Tull, Eric Clapton, Marianne Faithfull, John Lennon, Yoko Ono and five-year-old Julian Lennon. During 17 hours of recording, the "circus acts" performed various songs,

Above: The person dubbed the 'Zodiac Killer' wrote letters to the media after a series of murders in northern California between 1968 and 1970. The identity of the serial killer remains a mystery.

Right: After a dispute with their record company, the Rolling Stones finally released their *Beggars Banquet* album in December – and celebrated with a real-life banquet.

including an unofficial supergroup of Lennon, Clapton, Keith Richard and Mitch Mitchell – christened The Dirty Mac – performing 'Yer Blues'. Journalist Keith Altham attended the recording, and dubbed it the "most exciting pop show I have ever seen," and he was one of the few to see it, as it was never broadcast.

A couple of days earlier, the first "non-Beatles" album was released on Apple when American singer/songwriter James Taylor issued his eponymous debut album. Produced by the label's A&R chief, Peter Asher, the album failed to make any impression, and Taylor soon returned to the US, where he was eventually managed by Asher.

Meanwhile in Japan, Tokyo was the scene of a major bank robbery when a motor cyclist posing as a police officer made off with 300 million yen ($3.4 million) and was never seen again. Despite police interviewing over 118,000 people, they failed to make any arrests and the crime remains unsolved, and has inspired numerous TV shows and feature films.

The British musical film *Oliver!* written by Lionel Bart, directed by Carol Reed and starring Mark Lester and Ron Moody, premiered in America on December 11, ahead of it winning the Oscar for Best Picture. It was followed by another British musical movie, *Chitty Chitty Bang Bang*, opening in both the UK and the US. Based on a story by James Bond author Ian Fleming, and with a screenplay co-written by Roald Dahl, the film starred Dick Van Dyke and Sally Anne Howes.

Two American political dynasties were joined together when David Eisenhower (grandson of former President Dwight) married Julie Nixon (daughter of new President Richard) on December 22 in a New York church. The new Mrs Eisenhower explained, "Whether my father

Left: The Oscar for Best Picture went to Lionel Bart's musical *Oliver!* starring ten year-old Mark Lester.

Right: James Bond producer Albert Broccoli changed his tune to make the musical *Chitty Chitty Bang Bang*, written by Bond's creator Ian Fleming.

MARMALADE WIN THE RACE

On the back of their top-ten hit 'Loving Things' and a successful tour of Israel, Marmalade returned to their manager's office to hear the news that The Beatles' music publisher, Dick James, had "something special" for them.

Two members of the Scottish five-piece group – bass player Graham Knight and rhythm guitarist Pat Fairley – were dispatched to see James, as the band's lead guitarist Junior Campbell recounts. "He [James] gave them the shyster publisher blarney that 'the boys' [The Beatles] thought it would be great for us, and it would be exclusive to us."

The two members of the group returned with a white-label acetate of 'Ob-La-Di, Ob-La-Da', which they played to the rest of the group, including Dean Ford and Alan Whitehead. "Immediately I said 'that's The Beatles,'" recalls Campbell, who explains that they then sent a telegram to their manager, Peter Knight, who was in South America with The Tremeloes. "The reply came back that on no account should we cover a Beatles track, and two of the Trems also said we'd be nuts if we did."

Having been advised that The Beatles' new album was being released in late November, Marmalade attempted to co-ordinate their release and set about recording their version of McCartney's song. "Producer Mike Smith booked us in for an all-nighter at the CBS Studios on November 18," as Campbell explains, "but we were booked to appear in a club in Stockton on Tees for the week, so had to learn and rehearse the song up there, and then we flew to London on a private plane and took a cab to the studio."

After recording the song, Marmalade flew back to Stockton to finish their booking while the track was mixed and eventually released on December 4. "Then we learned the reality that Dick [James] had sold the same story to around another five bands, so the race was on," says Campbell.

McCartney has confirmed that he took the title for the song from a phrase used by Nigerian conga player Jimmy Scott-Emuakpor but, for Campbell, the name of Marmalade's biggest hit will forever be "Oobly Doobly" – "I've always called it that."

Their version – described by *NME* as having "just the right degree of sunshine and carefree abandon" – held the No. 1 spot in the UK for two weeks, sold a million copies and gave Marmalade the distinction of becoming the first Scottish group to top the British singles chart, while another band approached by Dick James, the Bedrocks, peaked at No. 20 with their version of the song.

Left: Marmalade's version of 'Ob-La-Di, Ob-La-Da' spent two weeks at the top of the charts in 1968.

BORN
British TV presenter Kate Humble (12)
Spanish singer Alejandro Sanz (18)
Danish model/actress Helena Christensen (25)

DIED
American film star Tallulah Bankhead (12)
World boxing champion Jess Willard (15)
Celebrated author John Steinbeck (20)

won or lost we had no desire to be married in the White House."

Two days before Christmas – and five years ahead of Pink Floyd's epic album – the manned space mission *Apollo 8* went to the dark side of the moon. During ten orbits, astronauts Frank Borman, Jim Lovell and William A Anders became the first humans to see the far side and witness an "earthrise".

The season of peace and goodwill to all men was shattered on December 28 when Israel's armed forces – in retaliation for an attack on an Israeli airliner – launched an attack on Lebanon's Beirut airport, destroying 12 passenger planes and two cargo planes valued at an estimated $43 million. There were no casualties in the raid, which was code named Operation Gift.

1969 – WHEN THE SWINGING SIXTIES CAME TO AN END

While the New Year began in familiar style with The Beatles once again topping charts on both sides of the Atlantic, change was in the air as the "fab four" fell out, and began to go their separate ways as love and peace suffered a death blow.

January opened with a host of Beatle developments as McCartney continued with his efforts to try to get the group back on stage – this time, after plans for a show at London's Roundhouse had faltered, there was talk of performing in a Roman amphitheatre in Tunisia. At the same time, 30,000 copies of Lennon and Ono's album *Two Virgins* were impounded by police in America, where the naked cover shot was deemed pornographic.

Two more new Beatles ventures also saw the light of day as the soundtrack to the animated film *Yellow Submarine* – with six tracks by The Beatles – was released, and the film *Wonderwall*, with music by George Harrison, came out.

At recording sessions for what would turn out to be the 1970 album *Let It Be*, Harrison, after falling out with both McCartney and Lennon, decided he had had enough and quit the group, only to return a few days later. On his return, all four Beatles met with US music manager and publisher Allen Klein to discuss business plans, and Harrison joined forces with Lennon and Starr to invite Klein to go through their financial records, while McCartney abstained.

On January 30, six days after students at the London School of Economics demonstrated over new security measures and the suspension of officials from the National Union of Students,

The Beatles played what would be their last-ever live show. With Billy Preston on organ, the group played for 42 minutes on the roof of their Apple offices in London's prestigious Savile Row until police, acting on a complaint about the noise, brought the lunch-time show to a halt.

February began with Yasser Arafat becoming head of the Palestine Liberation Organization. Meanwhile, Allen Klein was named as The Beatles business manager, while Lee Eastman and son John Eastman (father and brother of McCartney's girlfriend, Linda Eastman) were appointed as general counsel.

The month continued with a number of "firsts" – Boeing's 747 "jumbo jet" made its debut

flight in America, the US space probe *Mariner 6* set off for Mars and The Beatles began recording tracks for the album that would come out in October. 'I Want You', which would become 'I Want You (She's So Heavy)', was started in Abbey Road on February 22.

Another significant lift-off took place in France at the beginning of March, when the world's first supersonic airliner, *Concorde 1*, made its maiden test flight from an airfield in Toulouse, travelling for 27 minutes and reaching just 300mph. A month later, Britain's *Concorde 2* followed suit, and took off from Bristol for a 20-minute flight with a top speed of just 200mph.

Disillusioned with life with The Beatles after Brian Epstein's death, music publisher Dick James and his partner, Charles Silver, sold their shares in Northern Songs – the company which owned the rights to the Lennon/McCartney songbook – to Lew Grade's ATV company.

Around the time when Golda Meir became Israel's first woman Prime Minister, so McCartney and Eastman were joined in wedlock

---

Left: Allen Klein was named as The Beatles' manager in 1969, and took over handling the band's business affairs.

Above: Linda Eastman became Linda McCartney when she and Paul tied the knot in 1969.

at London's Marylebone Registry Office on March 12, just eight days ahead of Lennon and Ono getting spliced in Gibraltar. The couple were on the "rock" for just 70 minutes before jetting off to Amsterdam for a seven-day peace bed-in in the city's Hilton hotel.

The month ended with the death of former American President Dwight 'Ike' Eisenhower, who had led the US forces during World War II, and Scottish singer Lulu sharing in a four-way tie at the Eurovision Song Contest in Madrid. Her entry, 'Boom Bang-A-Bang', shared the top prize with entries from Holland, France and host nation Spain.

While The Beatles basked in the glory of 'Get Back' becoming their 16th UK No. 1 single, April also celebrated the *QE2* liner setting sail for the first time, travelling from Southampton to New York in four days and 16 hours. And, after ten years as President of France, Charles de Gaulle stood down to be succeeded by Georges Pompidou.

Having appointed Klein to be his manager – as had Starr and Harrison – John Lennon found that his American visa was being revoked following his earlier drug conviction, with US authorities suggesting it would only be renewed after "very serious consideration." All this coincided with Northern Songs finally being wholly acquired by ATV.

The ground-breaking film *Midnight Cowboy*, with Jon Voight and Dustin Hoffman, opened, featuring Nilsson's performance of the song 'Everybody's Talkin'. The US Government announced a phased withdrawal of troops from Vietnam, while American singing star Judy Garland was found dead in London from an accidental drug overdose.

May saw Jamaican reggae singer Max Romeo in trouble when his hit 'Wet Dream' was, perhaps not surprisingly, given a blanket ban by the BBC, who also instructed their disc jockeys never to mention the title (despite the fact that it reached the UK top ten), and simply refer to it as "a record by Max Romeo." The Beatles were also upsetting broadcasters in America and Australia when

they decided to ban 'The Ballad of John & Yoko', the group's last-ever UK No. 1, alleging that use of the word "Christ" was blasphemous.

A third record suffered a radio ban in the summer when the "suggestive noises" coming from Jane Birkin and Serge Gainsbourg (dubbed Jane Firkin & Surge Forward in *Private Eye* magazine) forced their July No. 3 hit 'Je T'Aime Moi Non Plus' off both *Top of the Pops* and Britain's radio programmes, while the record label Philips pulled copies out of the shops in the face of a media outcry. However, in October the record finally topped the UK chart, and earned a place in history as the first UK No. 1 not to be played on *Top of the Pops*.

July began with the news that Brian Jones, a founding member of the Rolling Stones, had been found dead in the swimming pool at his home in Sussex and, two days later, on June 5, the Stones dedicated their free concert in Hyde Park to his memory. Over 25,000 fans heard

Mick Jagger read a poem by Percy Bysshe Shelley before releasing a host of butterflies.

In the same month, British troops were deployed on the streets of Belfast following sectarian riots across Northern Ireland, while American Senator Edward Kennedy (brother of former President John F Kennedy) was at the centre of a police inquiry after Mary Jo Kopechne died when the car he was driving plunged into a river in Massachusetts. He received a two-month suspended prison sentence for leaving the scene of an accident.

The space race was finally won by America on July 21, when Neil Armstrong became the first man on the moon after *Apollo 11* landed in the Sea of Tranquillity. Edwin 'Buzz' Aldrin followed him on to the planet's surface while Michael Collins waited in the lunar module, *Eagle*. Over 600 million watched the event live on television, and the three astronauts returned to earth on July 24.

In the final week of the month, Elvis Presley returned to the stage for his first live concert since 1961, his 57 shows at the International Hotel in Las Vegas netting him $1.5 million. Just a week later, all four Beatles were assembled on the pedestrian crossing outside Abbey Road Studios in London by photographer Iain Macmillan, for a photo shoot for the cover of their next album.

Hippie Charles Manson was the leader of a sect in Los Angeles, and in August he sent his followers out to murder actress Sharon Tate and four others in a Hollywood house. He claimed he was inspired by the songs 'Helter Skelter', 'Rocky Racoon' and 'Piggies' from the White Album. Manson and three others were sentenced to death, but had their sentences commuted to life imprisonment, while Lennon commented that Manson was "barmy".

On the other side of America, thousands of hippies and music fans gathered in mid-August near Bethel in New York State for the first Woodstock Music & Art Fair, when the likes of Richie Havens, Joan Baez, The Who, Janis Joplin, Jefferson Airplane, Santana, Joe Cocker, Crosby Stills Nash & Young, Blood Sweat & Tears and Jimi Hendrix performed over four days to an estimated 450,000 people.

Just three weeks after their *Abbey Road* album-cover photo shoot, The Beatles assembled at John Lennon's home, Tittenhurst Park, for what would be their last group photograph. Meanwhile in the bigger world, Libya became a republic after Colonel Gadaffi led an army coup, North Vietnam's Communist leader Ho Chi Minh died, and American President Richard Nixon continued with bombing raids over North Vietnam.

A few days after performing on stage at Toronto's Varsity Stadium with his new Plastic Ono Band, Lennon apparently told his three fellow Beatles that he was leaving the group. The following week, the last album the band recorded together – *Abbey Road* – was released. It took the No. 1 spot in both the UK and the US for 11 weeks, and sold over four million copies worldwide in less than two months.

On the heels of the opening of film *Butch Cassidy and the Sundance Kid*, starring Paul Newman and Robert Redford, the extraordinary comedy series *Monty Python's Flying Circus* was seen for the first time on British television. Jack Kerouac, inspirational beat poet and author of *On the Road* and *Big Sur*, died aged 47, while 'Something', from *Abbey Road*, was released as the first Beatles' A-side not written by Lennon & McCartney. Harrison's song peaked at No. 4 in the UK, but hit No. 1 in America.

On the back of their free Hyde Park concert in London, the Rolling Stones ended their US concert tour with a free show at the Altamont Speedway track in California in December with San Francisco-based Hell's Angels employed as security guards. When fan Meredith Hunter waved a gun at the front of the stage, he was stabbed to death by the "Angels" amid chaotic scenes; three other fans were also killed in unrelated accidents.

Following the concert in Toronto, Lennon and his new Plastic Ono supergroup, featuring Eric Clapton, Keith Moon and Billy Preston, performed a "Peace For Christmas" concert at London's Lyceum Ballroom, while Harrison rounded off his year by joining Delaney and Bonnie for three shows in Copenhagen.

Finally, in a year when both *The Saint* and *The Avengers* came to an end on British TV, Jon Pertwee was named as the third Doctor Who, and Cream, The Moody Blues, Jethro Tull and Blind Faith all topped the albums chart for the first time. The Beatles brought the curtain down on their long-running series of freebie fan-club records, which began in 1963.

At the same time, the *Beatles Monthly* magazine, launched in 1963, also ceased publication after 77 issues, so maybe, with their seventh and final Christmas disc, 'Happy Christmas 1969', the "fab four" were sending us all a message that there were major changes on the horizon for both The Beatles and their fans.

Right: John Lennon and Yoko Ono perform with the Plastic Ono Band at the Lyceum Ballroom in London.

INDEX

BIBLIOGRAPHY

Tony Barrow, *John Paul George Ringo and Me* (Andre Deutsch 2006)

The Beatles, *The Beatles Anthology* (Cassell & Co 2000)

Fred Bronson, *Billboard Book of Number One Hits* (Billboard 1997)

Peter Brown & Steven Gaines, *The Love You Make: An Insider's Story of The Beatles* (McGraw-Hill 1983)

Tony Bramwell with Rosemary Kingsland, *Magical Mystery Tours: My Life With The Beatles* (Robson Books 2006)

Jeff Burger, *Lennon On Lennon* (Omnibus Press 2017)

Eric Clapton, *Eric Clapton: The Autobiography* (Century 2007)

Ray Coleman, *Lennon: The Definitive Biography* (Pan 1995)

Luke Crampton & Dafydd Rees, *Rock & Pop Year By Year* (Dorling Kindersley 2003)

Hunter Davies, *The Beatles Book* (Ebury Press 2016)

Geoff Emerick, *Here, There & Everywhere: My Life Recording The Beatles* (Gotham Books 2006)

Bob Harris, *Still Whispering After All These Years* (Michael O'Mara Books 2015)

Bill Harry, *The Beatles Encyclopedia* (Virgin Books 2000)

Dave Henderson *The Beatles Uncovered* (The Black Book Company 2000)

Spencer Leigh *Tomorrow Never Knows: The Beatles On Record* (Nirvana Books 2010)

Mark Lewisohn, *The Complete Beatles Recording Sessions* (Hamlyn 1988)

Mike Love, *Good Vibrations* (Faber & Faber 2016)

Nick Mason, *Inside Out: A Personal History of Pink Floyd* (Weidenfeld & Nicolson 2004)

Barry Miles, *The Beatles Diary* (Omnibus Press 1998)

Barry Miles, *Paul McCartney: Many Years From Now* (Secker & Warburg 1997)

Graham Nash, *Wild Tales* (Penguin 2014)

Craig Rosen, *Billboard Book of Number One Albums* (Billboard 1996)

Brian Southall, *Abbey Road: The Story of the World's Most Famous Recording Studio* (Patrick Stephens 1982)

Steve Turner, *A Hard Day's Write* (Carlton 2005)

Bob Woffinden, *The Beatles Apart* (Proteus Books 1981)

ACKNOWLEDGEMENTS

My thanks to go Roland Hall at Carlton Books for his support and ideas, and to all his colleagues who helped in bringing this book to fruition. They also go to all the people who gave up their time to share their recollections and opinions – both are much appreciated. Finally thanks to the British Library and its comprehensive collection of back issues including *Billboard*, *Melody Maker*, *Music Week*, *New Musical Express*, *Record Retailer*, *Crawdaddy*, *Rolling Stone* and *Q*, plus assorted national newspapers. I am also grateful to the websites: the whitealbumproject and BeatlesBible

CREDITS